STREAMWALKER'S JOURNEY

Other Books by Walt Franklin:

Beautiful Like a Mayfly
Wood Thrush Books
(personal essays)

River's Edge: A Fly-Fishing Realm
Wood Thrush Books
(personal essays)

A Rivertop Journal
Writers Publishing Cooperative
(personal essays)

Sand & Sage: The Trails Beyond
Great Elm Press
(personal essays)

The Singing Groves
Timberline Press
(essay)

Earthstars, Chanterelles, Destroying Angels
Foothills Publishing
poetry

Songscapes
Great Elm Press
(poetry)

Uplands Haunted by the Sea
Great Elm Press
(poetry)

The Wild Trout
Nightshade Press
(poetry)

STREAMWALKER'S JOURNEY

Fishing the Triple Divide

by

Walt Franklin

Wood Thrush Books

Published by: Wood Thrush Books
                   27 Maple Grove Estates
                   Swanton, Vermont 05488

ISBN 978-0-9903343-7-8

Acknowledgements

Parts of "A Slate Run Odyssey" were originally published on the website *Rivertop Rambles* and in *The Slate Drake*, the newsletter of the Slate Run Sportsmen in Slate Run, Pennsylvania (September 2013). The quoted sections of the essay are also by Walt Franklin, and they first appeared together as a chapter called "Slate Run" in the book *50 Best Places, Fly Fishing the Northeast* by Bob Mallard (Stonefly Press, 2015). "Slate Run" also appeared in digital format as *Fly Fishing Slate Run* by Walt Franklin (Stonefly Press, 2013).

Special thanks go out to the following individuals whose help assisted the production of this work in one capacity or another: James Cecilia, Tim Didas, Scott Cornett, Alyssa Franklin, Brent Franklin, Leighanne Franklin, Walt McLaughlin, Bob Stanton, and Jessie Vaughn.

The author also wishes to thank the many readers and supporters of *Rivertop Rambles*, his blog at **www.rivertoprambles.wordpress.com**, who helped inspire some of his outings in a quest for peace and an understanding of the natural world we live in.

Table Of Contents

Introduction: Three River Rise . . 9

The Triple Divide 11

Where Rivers Are Born . . . 18

Brook Trout Basics 27

A Slate Run Odyssey 43

Micro-Flyfishing 56

An Autumn Journal 64

A Creek with Almost Everything . . 75

Self-Portrait of the Fisherman as Idler . 85

Before and After Fly-Fishing . . . 98

Upper Kettle, Sunday 111

The King, the Spider, and the Rise . . 121

A Spring Creek Journal . . . 130

Blue Ridge Buffer 140

Water Dog 149

The Cedar Run Experience . . . 157

The Dream Cast (Night Flier) . . . 186

STREAMWALKER'S JOURNEY

Introduction: Three River Rise

Two of North America's major watershed divides meet at one location near my home along the New York/Pennsylvania border. Of the six primary watershed divides in North America, the two that lock together on a hill near Gold, Pennsylvania are called the St. Lawrence and the Eastern Continental divides. The hill near Gold, PA has a modest 2,502-foot elevation and is sometimes referred to as "Headwaters Mountain" or "Three River Rise" because of one significant fact: the summit has a triple watershed divide. The hill gives rise to three of my favorite trout streams—the Genesee River, the Allegheny River, and Pine Creek.

The Genesee River flows northward into New York State and empties into Lake Ontario, which eventually drains its content into the St. Lawrence River and the north Atlantic. The Allegheny River flows westerly from the hill for 325 miles to merge with the Monongahela in Pittsburgh, thus forming the great Ohio-Mississippi drainage to the Gulf of Mexico. Pine Creek has a southerly flow from Headwaters Mountain to join with the West Branch Susquehanna and, later, the Chesapeake Bay. Pine Creek, with its dramatic 87-

mile length, has been called "the biggest creek in the U.S.A."

The headwaters of these streams form the only triple divide point east of the Rocky Mountains. The only other triple divide in the U.S. is in Glacier National Park. Each of these three rivers forming on the hill near Gold, PA has a beauty all its own. The Genesee, at Letchworth State Park in New York, features the "Grand Canyon of the East." Pine Creek has an equally impressive canyon near Wellsboro, Pennsylvania. The westward flowing Allegheny has a stretch of "wild and scenic water." Collectively, these headwaters also form a great place for a trout-bumming, river-rambling person to explore.

Over my several decades of fly-fishing on these waters and paying attention to them by way of hiking and natural history studies, I have watched these streams and rivers rise in my thoughts and care. As a "streamwalker" in love with the outdoor life since boyhood, I saw my journey of exploration intensify after settling in this region in the 1980s. Since then I've been involved with an upstream ramble toward the sources of hundreds of streams in New York and Pennsylvania, as well as in states much farther afield.

All in all, it may have been a spiritual quest, of sorts. The journey has had its existential aspects, surely, but in every case I've wanted these experiences to be educational and fun. They have formed a major chapter in my book of life, a reading to be shared and hopefully enjoyed. Thankfully, this journey, often with a fly rod close at hand, remains a work in progress.

The Triple Divide

1

The triple divide of watersheds, unique to the eastern half of the United States, is a natural feature of my home ground where I like to explore and fly-fish for trout. Three large river systems are born on a hill near the hamlet of Gold, Pennsylvania and flow in separate directions, thus forming a major divide. The hill summit forms a common source for the Allegheny River, flowing westward to the Ohio and Mississippi rivers, for the Genesee River (Middle Branch) rippling northward through New York to Lake Ontario and the Atlantic, and for Pine Creek muscling up for its run to the West Branch Susquehanna and Chesapeake Bay. The triple divide remains a home for the beautiful char commonly referred to as the Eastern Brook Trout, or "brookie," *Salvelinus fontinalis*. The wild fish is an indicator species for my region, signifying a healthy environment when found in sufficient numbers, or telling of a stressed environment when absent.

For a casual exploration of the upper watersheds near Gold, I decided to choose three small streams, one for each of the river systems, and to walk them with a fly rod in hand. I began the series of visits in winter

11

when the season was relatively warm, allowing me a simplified black-and-white view of the environment with a minimum of distractions.

Pennsylvania has special fishing regulations in effect for die-hards like myself who like to keep active year around and, of course, these regulations need to be followed. Although many of the streams I fish are in state forest lands, some of them flow through private lands and do require landowner permission before an entry is made.

I began my series of visits to the big divide on the western slope of Headwaters Mountain where the Allegheny River gathers force. I stopped at a little feeder stream where a first black stonefly of the season flew up from the water and landed gently on the back of my hand.

The air was 30 degrees Fahrenheit and the water registered a cool 39. The stream was a little low and its color was clear. Despite my careful stalking, several brook trout scattered from the shallow pools. The narrow stream is a tough one to negotiate in winter, even more so in summer, when the banks and canopy are lush with growth. Nevertheless, this is a quality wild trout stream that has plenty of "structure" enabling fish to survive.

I worked my way upstream farther than I'd gone before, employing simple swing casts or a tricky bow-and-arrow shot into little enclaves underneath the branches. The afternoon solitude was enjoyable; the trout were excellent companions.

A brown trout surprised me when it gave a fearless chase of a drifting nymph. In a small stream such as this, a wild 13-incher on the line seems larger than life. And then, stepping out to the gravel camp road I encountered the tracks of a forest denizen, the bobcat. Each paw print of the cat was nearly the size of my fishing reel. To stand there by the tracks of this winter cat put me on edge, beyond the borders of a routine day. I could peer into the eyes of wildness and the living spirit of three river systems. I was at the rivertops, renewing the journey of a streamwalker as I've done each year now for at least three decades.

I could hope that proposals for industrial development here (most recently in the form of wind-powered turbines and for hydrofracking the gas locked deep below the earth's surface) don't overpower the growing concern for keeping the watersheds clean and healthy. I enjoy politics about as much as a kick in the groin but, in places like this, a growing affection for the land and water runs smack into politics nine times out of 10. If you care deeply for a place that gathers attention from opposing interests, you should fight for it–non-violently, of course. For now, though, I pushed away the work of politics as if it was merely a spider web across the face on a cool June morning.

The three young rivers seemed like the head, the heart, and the soul of a human being. I could see them as a fluid body that embraced an old streamwalker and his fly rod. With luck, they would do the same for generations of visitors to come.

2

The next day I swung over the divide and eased my way down the Pine Creek headwaters. The southward flowing Pine (considered by some outdoor enthusiasts to be the largest "creek" in the nation), like the Allegheny and the Genesee rivers, has its source on the farms and woodlots near Gold. About 20 miles downstream, Pine Creek enters its renowned gorge, a 50-mile "Grand Canyon of Pennsylvania" that a Federal Task Force in 1972 ranked as "one of the three most impressive gorge areas in the East."

It was another mild winter day with an air temperature in the low 30s. The forested hollow drained by this feeder stream felt refrigerated until I reached the stretches where a sunlit slope began to radiate warmth.

Even though I'd been fishing and exploring this area of the upper Pine for 25 years, I'd never visited this tributary before. I had crossed its lower end on the highway plenty of times and had known that trout could be found there, but I'd never stopped to take an actual look.

No matter where you live, no matter what your outdoor interests are, once you start exploring the land and water that you want to learn about, you start to reap rewards for your effort. Here on the upper Pine, the open woods and trout stream of the state forest land were good to me because I entered them with little expectation or mental baggage (easy for *me,* perhaps!). If I found anything to stimulate my curiosity, it was icing on the cake.

It didn't matter that the stream was disappointing from a fishing perspective. I caught one finger-length brook trout on a stonefly nymph and that was it. My angling strategies might have been winter dull, but I think the stream was lacking something, too. It had insufficient "structure," as fishery biologists might say. A minimum of pools, undercuts, rocks, debris—those places for a trout to shelter in, places from which they can dart to grab some passing morsel from the hills.

The woods were winter quiet, and the solitude was pleasurable and rare. I knew that the big forests of the Pine would unveil more tributaries to explore someday, and that on some of those feeder streams the fly-fishing would be very good, indeed. For now, the forest helped to stir some thoughts and feelings for a gray head who was happy that thoughts and feelings still could rise to the level of recognition. They were like a spring trout, maybe—still sluggish from the cold, but hungry for the hatching fly.

3

"The season isn't open yet, is it?"

In response to his question, I explained to the landowner of the Genesee rivertop that the fishing season for his stream lasted until the end of the month. To fish now was okay, but no trout could be taken out or killed. In a few days, the season would be over; there could be no fishing then until the regular season started up again in April. I took advantage of the mild February weather and received permission to cast on a lovely stretch of trout stream near the watershed divide. I thought about another issue that the Genesee River landowner discussed with me…

"Oh, you didn't know?" he had asked. "Yeah, they're fracking right up there," he said, pointing to the ridge a short distance away. "One spill, and all three watersheds could get a dose, myself included."

I had other things to think about. The sun appeared in the winter sky; I had one more stream to fish before the season ended, one more watershed to check before investigation of the great divide was done for now.

I needed an enjoyable experience to carry into tomorrow. There was no guarantee that the next day would be brighter.

Here was one watershed where the fishing may have improved over the years that I've known it. The remaining farmers in this valley are more likely than before to have the stream fenced off for cattle, more likely to allow brush and trees to flourish near the banks. Anglers seem more inclined to release their catches than they were two decades ago. The uppermost reaches of the stream are brook trout water, cool enough in summer to discourage the spread of brown and rainbow trout, the hatchery fish that are stocked in the remainder of Pennsylvania's Genesee.

On this last leg of my three-day swing through the triple divide, I was glad for the experience, for the challenge of low clear water and its shelf-ice that made my wading efforts difficult.

Beauty is where you find it, and what I found became apparent in the sun-lit hemlock trees, in the mystifying pools and cross-channel logs, and especially in a hefty old brook trout that I caught. The fish looked like a four-year-old male (a geezer by brook trout standards), as dark in its skin as my own hair was gray. This wild trout was probably a loner in that undercut pool fed by a riffle, and I handled it as gently and minimally as I dared. With luck, I might catch him again in spring.

Earlier I had seen a first northern shrike of the season flying over the fields. As I walked back to the car, I saw a red-tailed hawk soaring on the breezes. A raven cawed hoarsely as it flapped above the stream. Two starlings chittered from a dead tree in an open field, then mimicked a few notes of an Eastern bluebird, as well. Clearly the season was changing.

Where Rivers Are Born

1

I visited a jump-across stream that flows gently into a creek near home. There's a hole in that stream, a splashy pool that measures roughly five feet wide and three feet long. A month earlier I had seen the flash of a sizeable trout in that hole but didn't catch it. On this return I made a careful approach below the pool. Using a five-foot nine-inch fly rod and a bow cast underneath the overhanging branches, I convinced the wild trout, a native brookie, to seize the bead-head nymph. The colorful adult fish, measuring a full nine inches long, was a big one for this nameless little feeder stream in the upper Susquehanna watershed.

According to my topographic map, the brook has an intermittent flow, but the pool is probably there, diminished beyond recognition, even in our driest summers. I suspect that the native trout I caught and released there is a year-round resident of the pool. Its world is incredibly small, a five-foot pool that's ruled by fear and hunger, where bits of food sweep in sporadically and are swallowed in a bolt of motion, where a movement from the air above could be the rush of death from a paw or a long-pointed beak.

As far as we're able to surmise, the trout's world is a place of full awareness, differentiating the need to eat, to spawn, and to survive predations from above. The trout we pull from the water with a hook and line will not be eaten (unless hunger is an overriding factor) but its beauty is a full reflection of a pristine world that satisfies the soul.

The place where rivers are born consists of a big family of waters that I've adopted or have been adopted by throughout my years of fly-fishing here. These are wild, cold streams and rivers that provide a reason to explore my life in the world, to seek out again and again those links between humanity and the infinite realm containing us.

I can stalk for trout along these banks and pools and eddies, sometimes pausing with the fly rod for a little speculation while looking here and there. Assuming the mantle of "streamwalker," I can exit from my box of habit and routine, from my tiny five-foot pool of life, to stretch out and to journey through a greater realm of creeks and rivers where the big fish swim, but even as I venture farther from the local water's source, I like to know that my anchor holds among the beautiful roots.

If I could hold the wooded hills and upland valleys of the Appalachian Mountain district of New York and Pennsylvania in my hands, they might look a little like the convoluted surface of a human brain. A portion of them might present a fine example of an eastern watershed divide, their summits staging the sources of renowned streams like Oswayo Creek, Rock Creek, West Branch Genesee, and West Branch Pine, to name a few. These are my home waters and, like anyone's favorite set of fishing holes, they can exercise imagination and develop needed angling skills.

Why should any of these headwaters, these newly born streams and rivers, matter in the scheme of modern life beyond one's personal preference for the peace and beauty they instill? The way I see it, the health of a region starts here where the planet's water has been cooled and purified. The water has been reissued here and given another chance to benefit human being, plant and animal. Because of this, and more, I'm drawn to the place where rivers are born to flow again. I'll meet with the unending presence of clean water, with its spirit in the form of wild fish and countryside. In the place where rivers are born I know I am not yet dying.

2

I doubt that much ever became of H.D. Thoreau's suggestion that every large town or watershed in the country preserve a piece of its best wild nature, especially in places near our population centers. A designated wild place, whether it be something as simple as a city or county park or as complicated as the preservation of a wilderness, could allow for the survival of threatened plants and animals and assist our own species in the maintenance of a healthy relationship with the wild. Although we're fortunate to have some wonderful parks and wild areas set aside forever in America and in the world, we haven't yet given our naturalists like Thoreau and John Muir much regard when it comes to the subject of preserving special locales near home.

My local watershed, the upper Genesee River, isn't particularly noted for its wild condition. Agriculture, resource extraction and small businesses have taken most of what was wild in the borderlands between New York and Pennsylvania. One or two wild remnants do remain, however, in the upper Genesee country. The wildest of these remnants is about three-square miles in size. It's a heavily forested tract that's drained by a small trout stream, one of the healthiest tributaries in the upper 40 miles of the Genesee. You'll forgive me, please, if I'm not too exact about its actual location. A jeep trail connects the chunks of private property here, the legal claims of sportsmen living in distant places. Headwater streams like this one wouldn't do well with a lot of fishing pressure.

I recently hiked the valley in March (when the fishing season was closed) to gain some insight into the valley on short notice. Lumbering had started over the winter months and I hoped it wasn't a prelude to horizontal hydrofracking for gas in the Marcellus Shale layers below. Several pipelines had already crossed the valley, one of them across the middle section and the others across the headwaters near the summit of a hill. Gas extraction has long produced a major impact on the region.

3

I've always loved the thin blue lines on topographic maps. I've enjoyed their free-form routes through hills and mountains that owe their existence to flowing water. I find that those squiggly blue lines suggest the poetry of nature, the spell cast by cold flowing streams.

Whether the lines represent a tumbling brook or a placid meadow stream, they always promise to be small and intimate enough to hint of sprawling mysteries and dream.

I was first drawn to a blue line on a topographic map before I had reached my teens. A swamp lay between two wooded hills near the house where I was living. The swamp was located close enough for a kid to get acquainted with its possibilities. A lonely country boy in the middle of the twentieth century had time for things such as hills and swamps, and I became fascinated with a detailed map that indicated an outlet for the swamp, a thin blue line that led to new places for my rambling hikes. I had to imagine what the countryside was like on either side of that mysterious blue signature. Although I never got a chance to follow the swamp's outlet very far because my family suddenly decided to move hundreds of miles away, I've found, in retrospect, that the blue line of youth led to hundreds of other streams or brooks on topographic maps throughout the years, an inland country of headwaters and rocky ground where rivers are always in the process of being born.

An important feature of the blue line that attracts me is the possibility of finding native trout there. In the country of the "three river rise," the species that stirs imagination for the angler is the native brook trout.

Many of the area's small streams that I've fished over the years have a name appearing on a local map, but others have no name that I'm aware of. These headwater streams may range in size from "jump-across" to 10 or 12 feet wide. Unfortunately, too many of them no longer hold native trout, the eastern char, *Salvelinus fontinalis*. In a vain attempt to offset the loss of trout streams throughout the species' original range, I'm always searching far and wide for a new blue line to explore.

4

I walked downhill from the country road to the stream that flows from a major summit and has no camps or homes or farms along its banks. Although this blue line waterway is less than six miles from my home and holds a remnant brook trout population, I had never fished it for some odd reason. I'd assumed that the stream was on private property, and so was off limits and probably uninteresting. I'd been concentrating my angling energies elsewhere and had failed to recognize the full potential of a trout stream close to home.

To see and to experience this little creek, or brook, I had to shake my head. How had I managed to ignore it all these years? After thinking I had seen and fished all the promising flows within a 10-mile radius of home, I was looking at a whole new world. It wasn't the first time that I'd made a back-yard discovery on this scale. Whatever had led me to the place now reinforced the notion that streams and rivers draw me to them like a water droplet, and that streams and rivers have no end or limitations.

I rolled an artificial nymph into a little plunge pool of the stream. A first brook trout struck the fly about the same instant that I noticed a mink hunting its way quickly toward my location. The dark-furred predator darted in and out of nooks and crannies along the bank and made a sudden leap, almost snagging a tiny winter wren. Within five minutes, a second brook trout came to my hand and got released as I knelt by the plunge-pool like a foolish pilgrim in a magical land.

This stream is like other rushing brooks near home, small streams in a different watershed, but this one has a steeper gradient allowing the formation of numerous waterfalls. It has a flow that whispers "home water" in rock-tossed syllables that are louder and more succinct than the whispered songs of other regional streams. These waterways are all close to home, but this steeper flow contains a major difference—its source belongs to the same watershed as does the spring issuing water to my bathtub, sink and coffee brewer. This creek with its tumbling run says "home water" like no other, echoing with a sense of intimacy and friendliness that other streams fall short of. Its native trout are not abundant between the plunge-pools and the waterfalls, but they seem to welcome me—who would catch and then release them—as a room in my own house might welcome me to rest.

5

I was on a Pennsylvania Class A trout stream high up in the headwaters of Kettle Creek (yes, I often venture well beyond the immediate environs of the Triple Divide) following a long walk in hot and humid weather. I was trying to shake off an irritating cloud of gnats when I inadvertently flipped the line and leader into a miniature riffle of the stream. Wham! I had brook trout number one.

Fishing trips don't ordinarily commence in such a way, of course, but on this occasion, it seemed that every little pool had at least one brook trout eager for a surface bug. My casual exploration of this six to eight-foot wide stream began to offer some of the fastest trout fishing I'd ever experienced.

The forest environment intrigued me. There was no sign of human activity—no tires, no plastic, no aluminum, no boot print, nothing, and I hoped it would remain that way for a thousand years. To minimize my own impact on the stream, I put on the angling brakes after 30 minutes of careful stalking. Had I been crazier than usual and feeling good about myself, I probably could have caught a hundred trout in two miles of climbing but, clearly, it was time for self-restraint.

Sometimes your trout waters just flow serenely down the moments. You might revel in the fact that tumbling water sings an April song, no drama needed, while assisting your balancing act with the wild. There are challenges and they won't be easy to overcome. Your flies will get hung-up in the branches overhead or get snagged someplace else at the slightest loss of focus. And yet, the little stream may remind you of its stature in your life—how it helps you balance your domestic affairs, for example, with the broader scope of nature. Rivers are born between the mossy rocks of high ground but they're also born within the confines of the heart.

A streamwalker likes to think about the sources of the trout streams near his home or in an area which he enjoys visiting. White Pine Run is one of those streams, a headwater feeding into a well-known trout stream in his angling world. It's a small stream fed by numerous springs and has an excellent gravel bed, with undercut banks and a consistent series of riffles and pools. Its south side is a steep forested slope, and its north side is flanked by miles of field and seldom-used pasture.

He would easily recognize the weather for what it is—beautiful for just about everything except trout fishing. He imagines it—the sky is blue; the air is crisp and comfortable. He's way back in a hollow of the rivertops; the fishing is very slow, then suddenly he gets a take on the Hare's-Ear nymph. The struggle is a brief, all-out battle that strains the leader tippet to the point of breaking. That's right, the trout gets away, but he was going to release it anyhow. It's time to leave, so he steps out from the stream and marks his progress by building a small rock cairn at the field's edge nearby. He promises himself that he'll return and pick up the slack from this point on. He desperately wants to continue. He wants to find at least one place where the little stream is born.

Brook Trout Basics

1

For some outdoorsmen, it was the first day of archery season in the woods of Pennsylvania, but for me it was a day for brook trout basics. I was on a favorite brookie stream with the forest brightening on the slopes around me and with the colors of native trout intensifying with the spawn. The morning sun had disappeared, and by noon I was stalking like a heron through "a season of mists and mellow fruitfulness."

The creek, clear and cool at 49 degrees, was flowing at a normal pace. Brown caddis hatched sporadically. The day seemed perfect for my work with a seven-foot fly rod and a #14 Elk Hair Caddis tied to a tapered leader. I worked upstream slowly through a series of pools and riffles, making long casts where the opened banks allowed, dropping roll casts and bow-and-arrow shots where the boulders, logs and undercuts gave promise.

I recalled it was the birthday of my father who died a few winters earlier. I wasn't sure what triggered the memory but I reasoned that the misty hours and their colorful accents might have spurred the recollection. My father wasn't a fisherman but he loved the rural life and he taught me a few things early on. I was seven-years-old when he explained the wonders of bird migration and the beauty of tiny creatures called wood warblers. I'd be lucky to learn of them, and I never forgot. Perhaps Blackburnian, yellow-rump, Canada, and other warbler species had lent their migratory colors to the hues and patterns of the brook trout in my mind.

The trout action kept my thoughts in line and my eyes focused on the water. At a camp location where a spur of the Susquehannock Trail connects the stream to the valley heights, I found a wood turtle basking in the warmth of mud and autumn grasses. Would it mind if I placed it on a nearby picnic table for a photograph? The turtle didn't seem to mind its change of place but it did withdraw its head from my view.

Less shy was a green heron I encountered later in the afternoon. I was pulling in the tiniest brook trout in all of Penn's Woods when the heron, unbeknownst to me, flew out from a bank of tall grass and nearly grabbed the infant trout before sighting me and pivoting downstream. Herons are not typically a threat to healthy trout populations, although a lot of anglers might think otherwise. Maybe the fishermen are jealous of the long eye and the dominant, infallible beak, but think of it—herons and trout have evolved together for eons. If we want to worry about a threat to trout stability, we'd do better to become involved with slowing down man-made climate change and, on a local level, run-away hydrofracking operations for the gas inside layers of Marcellus and Utica shales.

Herons, turtles, warblers, witch-hazel blooms—they were all a part of brook trout fishing on a day in late September. A dozen brook trout rose to that singular caddis dry fly, and a dozen trout returned to their haunts in the upper Pine Creek watershed. It was good brook trout economics and a very good exchange.

2

I stopped one spring morning at a little stream a few miles from home. I hadn't fished the stream in six months and I had to find out if the brookies were okay. I stopped in with a fly rod and reel, as if checking in with an elderly parent, making sure the parent was alright and not lying on the floor. No doubt the brook trout were okay and had survived an average northern winter with no major casualties. But wait a minute… Were the trout really in good form?

To know for sure, I had to check in at Brook Trout Manor, the modest foothill home of native trout. I had to knock on the trouts' door and see who was in. I had to *catch* a trout, look it over then release it. That would be the medicine needed to begin a new angling season on a bright, sane note.

My casting to the first plunge-pool of a waterfall was not productive. Heading upstream into the woods, I glanced at the sky. Rain clouds were forming heavily and promising some needed rain. The streams were still low and clear. The local towns had burn bans in effect. I didn't know it yet, but we were in for heavy rainfall that would raise the streams to flood level in just a day or two.

I caught a year-old brookie in a small pool off the main current and then approached the second plunge-pool, my favorite holding spot on the creek.

With a second or third cast of the weighted nymph I had a fat brook trout on the line. I held the fish out in front of me for a moment, then released it. Things were looking better, and the rain began to fall.

Five days later I checked on another headwater stream, a project water for our Trout Unlimited chapter, and one of my favorite brooks for angling. Parking where the trout stream passes underneath the county road, I saw a couple of problems right away.

Unfenced cattle waded in the stream across the road; and down the bank from where I stood was a beaver dam, a new one. Beavers had moved onto this stream about a year earlier and, as far as native trout are concerned, there went the neighborhood—there went the spawning grounds.

Upstream, the original dam remains a massive affair, built across a stream that averages six to 10 feet wide. A few years prior I had organized a TU willow planting project for the stream banks, and now most of the planted trees were under water.

I found five or six new dams on this half-mile stretch of aging farmland. The full reservoir behind the bow-shaped original dam was spilling out of one side and pouring through the meadow. The new stream was eroding the fresh soil and dumping it back into the original creek bed after it rejoined. The gravel beds, the spawning ground, for brook trout were being smothered with deepening silt.

I used to like the beaver (and still do)—when their numbers were controlled by trappers and other environmental constraints. I encouraged their presence and wished them well. Now they seem ubiquitous as people. Their predators are gone. They've proliferated like deer in Steuben County where I live. I like most of them individually, but collectively they're as bothersome as a right-wing political party. If it's not hydrofracking or climate change or a host of other issues putting the screws on native trout and other species dependent on cold water, there are beaver in the mix.

I headed upstream, looking for better news. There the land is wilder and less supportive of the beaver industry. Trout Unlimited and New York's Department of Environmental Conservation (NYDEC) have built some in-stream structures there for trout. The habitat was given a helping hand to recover from losses incurred during the previous century. Our work sites are a source of pride.

I caught and released a young-of-year (yoy) brook trout at the first structure. At site number two, I brought in a beautiful, brightly colored male that slipped back into the stream before I could get his picture with the little camera I carried in my vest.

See ya! said the old guy, lord of his manor, as he splashed and shot away. "I'll see you, too!" I thought, as if just visited by an emissary from another world. "I'll see you if I'm lucky. Please drop by again!"

3

Okay, about brook trout and beaver dams... Let's start with a local stream called Vandermark Creek.

The Vandermark is a trout stream feeding the upper Genesee River in western New York. I have fished the headwater section of the creek occasionally over a period of several decades, particularly for native brook trout in and around the Vandermark State Forest. The upper creek is surrounded by a mix of woodland and aging fields and has remained basically stable throughout the time that I have known it. Over the past decade, however, I've seen a marked decline in its brook trout numbers, and I have a theory as to why.

I don't know when beaver came to be employed at the state forest, but the rodent engineers are there, and they're rocking the ecology of the woods. You might wonder if that's truly important. You might question the implications, considering bigger threats to native trout today, say, with hydrofracking, silt accumulation, global warming, etcetera. Why worry about a mammal that's evolved with brook trout over the ages? Granted, the eastern char has a lot to be concerned about today, but let's not disregard the beaver.

Castor canadensis may have evolved naturally with brook trout on a multitude of eastern streams but, remember, the trout's current range is a mere fraction of what it was in pre-colonial days, and the presence of expanding beaver colonies on a single brook trout water can have a major impact, especially if poor land use by our own kind has already minimized the number of fish.

My introduction to Vandermark Creek came long ago, during my Alfred University days in the 1970s. Since then I've never caught more than two trout at a single outing there, and I've never fished downstream for the brown trout that are stocked on a minimal basis every year. The creek has never seemed all that good for fishing, though I did manage to land a nice 11-inch wild brook trout on the stream a few years back. My last two outings at the creek were unsuccessful, and on a recent winter morning I inspected the low, clear waters and saw little more than beaver dams, silt and large quantities of chubs.

As the value of beaver fur has lessened over the past few decades, minimizing trapper interest, beaver populations have surged in many rural areas. The Avery Report, a study published in 1992, collected data from the impact of beaver colonies on trout streams in Wisconsin. The report had studied fish and mammal numbers before and after the removal of beaver dams on trout streams. After looking at streams for six years following the removal of dams, the authors of the Avery Report concluded that brook trout numbers rose and that water temperatures cooled. Stream turbidity was reduced; gravel beds were again exposed, allowing the spawning process to proceed. The flow rate of streams increased; the depth of water and the channel widths decreased.

Unfortunately, across the study area in the 1980s, summer air temperatures were higher than normal, thus the water temperatures of the streams where dams had been removed were cooler by an average of only two degrees Celsius. Considering the potential effect of global warming on native trout streams, conclusions from the studies of dam removal do not sound encouraging. As one report suggested, "air temperature is the most important element in controlling trout habitat."

I saw many little beaver dams in various conditions along the creek, and though I briefly fantasized that the beavers could be discouraged and the dams could be removed by hand, I wondered whose army would assist me if I felt comfortable messing around with nature, which I clearly wasn't comfortable with, given the unbalanced conditions in this ecosystem. It would be nice to see the sediment cleared away and to know that oxygen levels would be increased, but it would also be nice to see the whole human world living together in peace and harmony. It wasn't about to happen any time soon.

It's a different story in our western states. For example, beaver ponds in the Rocky Mountains often have an opposite effect on trout. The ponds allow herbaceous plants to grow, eventually adding to the food supply. But there we're talking about water temperatures rising from the 40s into the 50s under harsh conditions, rather than rising from the 50s or 60s into the 70s or beyond. Western ponds tend to have short life spans for fishing opportunities, but some of them, as difficult as they can be for maneuverability, offer a chance for good angling. It's possible that the fastest brook trout fishing I ever experienced was on several beaver ponds of the Colorado Rockies.

I asked Scott Cornett, fisheries biologist with the NYDEC in western New York, to reflect on beaver ponds and eastern trout streams, and Cornett replied, in part, "Most of our streams have become marginal temperature-wise for brookies due to our poor land use practices, and the beaver ponds just push them over the edge." He went on to say that new beaver ponds occasionally allow good trout fishing, but they quickly become silted in. As beavers rapidly consume the nearby wood supply, the waters warm up to allow, at best, the spread of brown trout in the watershed.

The beaver is an interesting rodent and the native brook trout is a beautiful char. Ordinarily the two can live together harmoniously as nature intended. When an ecosystem is unbalanced, the harmony starts to fray and tatter. I don't know what can be done about the problem, if anything, other than becoming more aware of what is out there in the wild and then encouraging the best land use practices available.

4

Redfern Creek (not its actual name) is a small, remote stream in the upper drainage of my home river and, in terms of my fishing experience, has been regarded as something of a last frontier. It was the last significant tributary of the upper river in New York State from which I hadn't yet caught a brook trout.

After the lumbering carnage of the early twentieth century, followed by the rapid rise of agriculture and other forms of land use in the region, Redfern was one of only several streams in my area whose brook trout population continued to flourish for a while.

But something detrimental happened after the lumbering era started to decline. According to recent reports from conservation officials and older fishermen, there was an occurrence, natural or otherwise, that caused this stream and others like it to lose significant portions of their volume, to become diminished in their flow rates and, not inconsequentially, to cause their fishing to go south.

My several previous attempts to catch a native trout in Redfern Creek were fruitless. Granted, the stream is an obscure blue line on the topographic map, a squiggle with resurgent forest cover, but it just didn't look like a home for brook trout. The stream is tiny, averaging five to nine feet wide, mostly shallow and without the kind of pools and undercuts preferred by native trout in hilly or mountainous terrain.

On a cool, spring morning in May, I decided to revisit Redfern for one last inspection, to see if I could finally locate a brook trout and to state with confidence that the water was alive.

I parked on a rough seasonal road and dropped down to the stream, as I've done in the past. The access is difficult here; an angler needs permission from the timber/mining corporation that owns the land, and then needs to be prepared for a bushwhack.

I was armed with a 5'9" three-weight rod and a short-tapered leader, plus a weighted fly. There was frost in the valleys, and the prospect for dry fly action, as sweet as that could be, was dim.

The first half-mile of water looked familiar— shallow, flood-torn, and peppered with the detritus of industrialism—old tires, bottles, shards of plastic— washed down from the road. But I'm glad I didn't quit the trek on this occasion.

The forest became more attractive. Foamflower and wild geranium colored the floor. Vireos and ovenbirds lent an auditory dimension to the heights above the stream. I finally found a little pool with some depth, but its roof of fallen trees prevented a traditional cast. I made a bow cast through an open window and the fly plopped into the center of the pool. A sizeable trout took it but quickly twisted free. Damn! Another lost opportunity? My *almost* link to Redfern Creek?

Ordinarily I would have moved on, but this pool might be the only one I'd find, so I waited several minutes and tied on a different fly.

The trout took again, and I pulled him out—a hemlock-colored native more than seven inches long, a small fish but a nice adult from a tiny feeder stream in rivertop country. So, what does this mean, to catch a singular fellow in a stream that might otherwise be totally devoid of fish? Could Trout Unlimited establish a rehab project there to help improve the habitat for trout, or should everyone just keep their hands off the place and let nature take its course as it has done for many years?

Granted, my little survey of the stream was amateurish, but it's given me a fresh look at its flow. The water looks to be a microcosm of the trout's world—as it was before the days of European settlement and as it is today. It speaks of both diminishment and hope.

5

Here's my take on how it's possible to step off the wheel of time while fly-fishing for trout and then reflecting on what's happened. I doubt if anyone can really step off the Big Wheel of Existence without dying in the process, but here's my suggestion for how one might *slow things down* while just enjoying life…

If you're like me, you hit the home water at the peak of the fly-fishing season. Here in New York/Pennsylvania that's about the middle of May until the middle of June, the exact times variant on seasonal conditions. You hit it during the full frenzy of the mayfly, caddis and stonefly hatches while the woods are greening, the spring wildflowers are taking color, and the bird song is at its sexual fullest. You take friends and family with you into the fly-fishing world (if the folks will allow you some solitude and casting space when needed). You enter it as if it was Heaven on Earth, stepping off the wheel of days and months and years and never wanting to leave. I don't know if you're as crazy about this season as I am once I'm in it, but I thought I'd mention the procedure anyway.

In the months of May and June, I can often be found on the Happy Fishing Waters of New York and Pennsylvania. At another time and place, let's say October on a different trout stream of the region, I can wax exuberant about the beauty of *that* turning season, as well, but for now it's springtime in an evening on a home stream with a mayfly hatch, and I'm loaded for trout and living.

The stream is in great condition, a little cloudy from the heavy rainfall of a day ago, with the water excellent for dry fly angling. Mayflies copied by a Light Cahill #12 begin to hatch, and the trout are hungry. I wade upstream slowly, casually, and pick up trout after trout. The population of wild trout seems to be at its peak for the stream. I tally eight wild brookies (average length seven inches), 10 wild browns (mostly small), a stocked brown, and four stocked rainbows (the largest at 14 inches). Not bad for a little headwater stream near the PA/NY border. Not bad for an old guy stumbling out of the woods at dusk with birdsong in his ears, and brook trout in his heart.

6

Trout Brook (not its real name, of course) is found within a few miles of where I live and is an excellent stream inhabited by native trout. Rocks and waterfalls break the lower half of Trout Brook's flow from a ridge between two major watersheds. For an hour or two each day after work, I fished along a mile of Trout Brook's water where no less than eight small waterfalls and plunge-pools can be found. Brook trout hide among the pools and were eager to rise and strike a drifting fly.

May is a terrific time to fly-fish in the Northeast and mid-Atlantic regions of the country and I hate to see a day go by unable to fish where the flies are hatching and the brook trout rising. Getting out there, by hook or crook (wading staff?), allows me to sustain myself and feel alive. I try to fish a little every afternoon, as much as I try to commute to work and back, to eat a decent meal, to absorb good music and to write. It's therapeutic, I suppose.

On the first afternoon of my visits to Trout Brook, I found the water a little high and slightly turbid. I fished the first two waterfalls above the hunting cabins, getting a strike at a dry fly on my first cast, but then doing better with a bead-head nymph. I caught six brookies at the plunge-pools but did nothing in the shallow waters between them where the stream bed is primarily slate.

The second afternoon I saw another storm-threat building over the hilltops. Again, I was fishing with a seven-foot Phillipson bamboo, a three or four-weight rod reworked by Tom Maxwell, of Thomas & Thomas Rods fame. This rod, which I purchased second-hand for very little money considering the man who reconditioned it, was perfect for the stream at these conditions. I caught two more brookies at waterfall #3 as I worked my way upstream before the rain finally caught me and punctuated my therapy session with trout.

The third afternoon promised heavy rain to come (and when it did arrive late that night, it poured and overflowed the streams and rivers, a reminder of the climate chaos in the world). I hastened my adventure by returning to the stream where I had left it the day before. I fished to the next two waterfalls and found the creek to be in good flow, but the hemlocks crowded the surface on one side, and a rock wall crowded me on the other. The trees and wall form a tunnel of wildness that is difficult to fish.

There were trout in the pockets between these waterfalls. Most of the brookies that I caught took a dry fly at the plunge-pools. It was a relief to break out from the tunnel and arrive at a pool. At that point, I could stretch and stand again and not feel like a four-legged predator emerging from rocks and overhanging branches. I could execute a forward cast again.

Although many of our local streams got blown-out temporarily from ensuing rains, my three short spells of brook trout fishing after work would come in handy for me. They were like a satisfying meal or like a sermon given from the lip of a pretty waterfall. They would get me through a few rough days of no fishing at all. I knew that I'd be coming back soon; the other waterfalls were waiting.

7

Canyons are fascinating formations in the surface of the Earth. I've enjoyed hiking and fishing them for years. Canyons seem to be the geologic inverse of mountaintops, and exploring them seems like an immersion in the Earth whereas climbing the high peaks is more like an attempt to conquer a piece of the planet. Maybe canyons suit the humble explorer, and maybe mountains are more suited for the alpha soul, although a canyon hike and a mountain climb both have elements of danger and beauty, so accomplishing either one is no kindergarten graduation. Entering a canyon is even better when I know that native trout dwell in its drainage.

The Pine Creek Canyon (or Gorge) of north-central Pennsylvania, one of the finest examples of a river canyon in the eastern U.S., has been a draw for me since the 1970s. On my initial descent into the canyon from Colton Point State Park, I saw the first black bear I ever encountered. Since then, every time I've entered a canyon, the phenomena of nature have presented themselves in some form or another and reflected new and fascinating light.

Recently I descended a side canyon of Pine, with fishing garb, containers of food and water, and a fly rod and reel. It was time to reacquaint myself with the splendid colors of brook trout living in a hanging valley of the Pine Creek drainage.

I was roughly a thousand feet below the Rim Trail of the Pine Creek Gorge, and fishing my way up a small tributary of Pine, a river popular for rafting, hiking, fishing, hunting, biking, and nature studies.

Popular, but not without its share of wildness where it's easy for an angler to fish in solitude and splendor. On this occasion, fishing between waterfalls on a beautiful brook trout stream with ferny seeps and mossy sidewalls, I saw no more than two other hikers all day, although the trout were rising and the air was springtime clear.

Again, the stage was set, and all the basics were in place.

A Slate Run Odyssey

1

The year 2011 was becoming one of the wettest seasons on record, but Slate Run wasn't fishing well, and its wild trout population seemed inexplicably low. The Slate Run Sportsmen (SRS) group, which I've supported with a membership for years, requested that the Pennsylvania Fish and Boat Commission (PFBC) conduct an electro-survey of the stream to hopefully provide some answers to pressing questions about the run.

In late 2011 I decided to fly-fish the entirety of Slate Run over a one-year period. I'd been fishing the run sporadically for 25 years (it's located two hours from home) but now I wanted to cover its 7.5-mile length from mouth to source, from Pine Creek to the junction of the Francis and Cushman branches. I wanted an angler's in-depth view, a personal counterpoint to the scientific survey to be given by the PFBC.

At the fall meeting of the SRS, my wife Leighanne won a rod and reel raffle sponsored by the group and the Slate Run Tackle Shop. The raffle would benefit an excellent cause—assessment of regional wild trout streams at risk from the Marcellus gas-production boom. Leighanne won the Orvis rod and reel, but doesn't fish, so someone had to test drive her new tackle. I stepped up to the plate like the fishing batter that I am and volunteered to use it on the looming Slate Run odyssey.

Following the raffle at the autumn meeting of the club, I took the four-piece, seven-foot Superfine model, with its new Orvis reel and four-weight line, to the mouth of Slate Run and started casting. Leighanne was watching from the bank and, by the time I passed the Hotel Manor a hundred feet upstream, she was witness to my first brown trout caught and released with the newly won rig. My caddis dry fly, attached to a long-tapered leader, was laid out with such ease that I knew I wanted the rod to accompany me for the whole length of the run. As my wife turned away and walked back to the hotel for a drink, I glanced again at the description found at the butt of the rod: "2011 Pine Creek Watershed Conservation Rod." Already the tool felt like an extension of my casting arm. I was on my way.

At last, after a year of heavy rains interspersed with a period of drought, Slate Run was looking good, its full-flowing water registering 58 degrees Fahrenheit. I noted several blow-downs from a June tornado. Working up to the Mowry Pool (the old "Swimming Hole") I caught and released several wild fish including a brightly colored eight-inch brookie. Who said there weren't any trout left in this renowned freestone creek? At the Mowry Pool, I saw dozens of fish, many of them trout, darting through the limpid flow. Ah yes, wild fish in a wild locale. They made this water special.

2

"Slate Run flows through the rugged mountains of northern Pennsylvania. The stream is named for its layers of slate outcroppings that stair-step downward from a high source to its mouth at Pine Creek. The run flows through a deep gorge with forest-covered slopes. The steep gradient, plus layers of slate, facilitate the formation of rocky pools, riffles, pockets, and underwater ledges inhabited by trout.

The first European settler in the Slate Run area was Jacob Tomb. He built a home, along with a sawmill and a gristmill, at the stream's mouth in the late 1700s. Other pioneers arrived soon afterward and homesteaded in the Pine Creek Valley. By the mid-1800s, the village of Slate Run included a general store, hotel, post office, and churches. A few decades later it evolved into a busy logging community—a far cry from its status as a haven for recreational activities in the twenty-first century.

Slate Run is categorized by Pennsylvania as a Class A Wild Trout Stream, one of the finest in the Northeast region. To recognize the stream as such in a state known for its premier limestone water speaks volumes. The Pennsylvania Fish and Boat Commission restricts angling at Slate Run to catch and release, fly-

fishing only. Trout Unlimited has ranked Slate Run as one of the top 100 trout streams in the United States. The stream flows entirely through public land, including two state forests, providing good access for the hiker and the fly-fisher.

Slate Run originates at the confluence of Francis Branch and Cushman Branch. After tumbling 7.5 miles through a canyon, it empties into Pine Creek near the village of Slate Run. It gathers additional water from several major tributaries—Red Run, Morris Run, and Manor Fork. These freestone streams are home to native brook trout and numerous wild browns. For the most part, the stream is paralleled by a road. In the case of many Eastern streams, such a road would provide easy access to the water. This is not the case, however, with Slate Run. Whereas the road will get you into the mountains, it is often hundreds of precipitous feet above the streambed and, not surprisingly, this makes access to Slate Run rather difficult…"

3

In October I left word with Jed Grove at the tackle shop that I'd be fishing from the Mowry Pool up to the Two-Mile access. Every walk had to be sequential, starting from where I'd left off on a previous outing. Six hours would be plenty of time to fish, but if I didn't report back to the tackle shop by 3 p.m., well, maybe I'd broken a leg somewhere in the gorge, or maybe I'd decided to abandon civilization altogether.

I found heavy water from previous rains, and Slate was flowing high and clear. I was glad to have a wading staff for support. In the morning fog, the water temperature was 52 degrees. Later, under a sunny afternoon sky, the stream's temperature would rise only a degree or two. I decided to cast dry flies and wet flies alternately, a decision I would later regret. In recent weeks, I'd been tying soft-hackled flies in earnest, and I was eager to try some of these old classic patterns. They would not produce well today. I began to wish I'd brought along my fly box that contained Slate Run favorites like the bead-head Hare's Ear Nymph and that elemental curiosity, the Green Weenie.

As I stumbled through the turbulent waters and watched the sun burn slowly through the fog, I encountered the first of many blow-downs from the June tornado. Great white pines and sycamores had fallen in a swath from north to south across the run. A flock of turkeys flushed from the welter as if the run had suddenly sprouted wings. Difficulties aside, the stream was looking good, with pocket water, pools and undercuts, with structure loved by trout and fishermen.

The air was warming, and the steep southern mountainside often kept me in the shadows. Everything seemed right with the world, with one exception—the trout were tight-lipped and shy about rising to my expectations on this walk.

At the Crooked Tree Pool, I recognized the bent hemlock and thought it less distinctive than in years gone by. The tree probably thought the same about me…

At a fire-ring beside the pool, I found unwanted remains of a camporee—bucket, chair, tarp, discarded cans of beer. As the designated "stream warden" for the Slate Run Sportsmen, I felt obligated to arrange a cleanup of the site for next spring.

With five hours of fishing under my belt, I had managed only half the distance to my exit at the Two-Mile post. Rushing forward, I felt the run push back, a slippery force that was looking much larger than its topographic map suggested! I had to get back before dark, had to be extra careful with my footing on the slippery rocks, and had to stay calm when the stream bends and mountain flanks appeared like gateways to eternity.

Beyond the Crooked Tree I found a couple of rock-lined pools with dripping sides. The Rock Pool struck me as a favorite stop between the Mowry Pool and the Two-Mile Hole, but despite some careful casting there, the trout weren't taking. It was one of those days. I remembered a remark by fishing guide Rich Meyers when we spoke long ago about Slate Run while drinking beers at the Hotel Manor. Rich said, "When Slate is on, it's great, but when it's off, it's really dead."

I proceeded hastily, and the twists and turns of the run became a little tedious. I was feeling humbled and small. It was good, though, to walk a crooked line between two worlds, to be balanced between wild nature and the human realm.

I wondered if a so-called "trout bum," that proverbial modern rebel, lives for moments of escape on the stream. If so, what does he or she escape from? Was it a life of quiet desperation, as Thoreau had envisioned? Maybe. I decided that, like many others, I enjoy escaping from the madness of civilization, but am quick to acknowledge there is no enlightenment here, no Zen stick rapping the skull for instantaneous wisdom and bliss.

I was happy to be far from speeding vehicles and their slave commitments, far from mountaintop communication towers, far from village traffic jams when the hydrofracking trucks roll through. I understood that escape is temporary, that escape is an immersion in wild nature, in the wide and brutal undercurrents of what is. The entry may be beautiful on the surface, but the push and pull on a mortal being must be respected and dealt with carefully.

A declining slope was bathed in sunlight and promise. It reminded me of the Two-Mile access trail but I wasn't sure if that was it. A pool that I approached was vaguely reminiscent of the Two Mile that I fished five or 10 years before. I figured I was getting close, so I quickened the pace and cut back on the casting. When I reached a deep, expansive pool, I thought of the Frying Pan, one of Slate Run's largest and finest holes.

I peered into its dream-like clarity and wondered if I'd missed my exit. I made several perfunctory casts and wondered where I was (indeed, the Pan must have clubbed me over the head till I was senseless). Only when I saw the massive rock ledge and the mouth of a tributary did I recognize my whereabouts. The Manor Fork! The well-known lodge was hidden up there in the trees. Today an idiot had missed his Two-Mile exit and had forged on to the Manor Fork, a trout stream tumbling in from the west.

I climbed from the gorge and headed up the driveway that connects the lodge to the Slate Run Road. A van was parked at the lot and I saw a motion at its opened rear. I offered a greeting and a quick explanation of my predicament. I heard a woman tell me she was changing her clothes. Whoops… Unless I got lucky and could hitch a ride along the roadway, there would be miles to walk before I could sleep.

I paused for a dead copperhead on the road. Only a foot in length. With a pit viper head and copper cross-bands on the back, it looked about the way I felt. When I finally saw my parked vehicle up ahead, the van with the woman in her fresh clothes drove by. It was 3:30 p.m. and I had walked the 3.5 road miles in less than an hour.

Hot and sweaty, I drank from a bottle and ate a snack, then changed my shirt and fishing gear. A vehicle approached, and I recognized Jed, from the tackle shop. Since I hadn't checked back at the shop as planned, Jed had thought to look for me on the road.

"I figured you might have missed the Two-Mile Trail," he said. I thanked him and explained how I'd gone troutless, messing around with new fly patterns when I should have stuck to the standards. That reminded us of the Green Weenie and how big trout in the run seem to fall for the pattern. Inch worms are a tasty morsel for the browns, or so it seems.

4

"... The best way to reach remote sections of the stream is to utilize the angler paths accessible from a half-dozen pull-offs on the road. Some of the easier access points are found at the Hotel Manor near the mouth of Slate, at the Two-Mile pull-off, at the Manor Lodge, and at the Morris Run Bridge (a dead-end road that's suitable for four-wheel drive).

Anglers should note that climbing back up to the roadway can be a challenge, so plan accordingly. During late spring and summer, timber rattlesnakes are always a possibility. While they seldom are a problem, pay attention and always give them plenty of room. Due to the rugged terrain and the wild nature of the gorge, it is never a bad idea to fish with someone else.

The upper section of Slate Run is a narrow mountain stream lined with boulders, evergreens, and deciduous forest. It consists of pocket water, riffles and small pools. Native brook trout are the predominant species here. An occasional brook may reach 12 inches long. Wild browns are also present but are smaller than their counterparts in the lower run. Slate's upper section receives less angling pressure than the lower stream, so the fishing may be more relaxing and the solitude more complete.

The lower half of Slate Run is primarily brown trout water, with fish generally larger than those encountered above. Browns of more than 20 inches in length are caught each year. During the summer, Pine Creek gets too warm for trout. Many of its fish then migrate into Slate Run looking for thermal refuge. These summer visitors settle into the lower stream and add to the resident fish population. Here the stream is wider and has longer pools and riffles, making it more hospitable to fly-casters. Areas close to Pine Creek may reach 30 feet or more in width.

The cool temperatures and fertile water found at Slate Run result in abundant hatches of mayfly, stonefly, and caddis. Even during the summer months, the water temperature remains cool enough for brook and brown trout. When other streams have become too warm for these cold-water creatures, angling on Slate Run continues to hold up well, providing summer recreation for the fly-fisher. The stream can be productive in any season, but winter fishing is not usually recommended due to the potential hazard of ice..."

5

In March I resumed the walk where I'd left off in the fall. I fished a Quill Gordon hatch to the Manor Falls Pool and wondered where the trout had gone. Winter had been unusually warm and dry; the streams were getting low already. I fished a while with my friend, Dale, and we found evidence of bait-fishing here on this fly-fishing-only water, but poaching, alone, could not account for the apparent scarcity of trout.

I was situated roughly at the mid-point of my journey up Slate Run from its mouth to its origin at the confluence of two branches. I basked in the knowledge that the stream was lovely here, remote, without a real beginning or end, a place beloved by many anglers far and wide. It was a wild place tumbling through the heart forever. There would be seven or eight more trips this year before I finally arrived at the Francis-Cushman Hole in October.

This spring my visits would be accompanied by songbirds such as the wood thrush and scarlet tanager. They would have the floral company of plants such as painted trillium and mountain laurel as I passed the tributaries of Red Run and Morris Run. I would find good insect activity in March Browns and Yellow Stoneflies at the Red Rock and White Rock pools.

By late August, Slate Run was extremely low as another dry season settled on the canyon. But we heard good news about the stream. The state survey team had come to Slate Run and the preliminary results of the electro-survey indicated that the trout were getting by. The brook trout numbers were minimal, perhaps due to the extreme weather conditions, the alternating high water and drought events, over the previous decade. A few large brown trout were examined, but the small ones, the young-of-the-year browns, were plentiful and promising.

I would change my fishing tactics to adapt to low-water conditions. When visiting the heart of the upper run, I would find tranquility and solitude. I'd reacquaint myself with pools named Dripping Ledge, Three-Quarter Mile, Washboard, Gargoyle, Beaver Pond, and Shady Rest. At one point, I hoped the trout couldn't read my t-shirt that displayed a large Royal Coachman and the words, "Don't Touch My Fly!"

I would note once more that Slate, with its gorge and its wonderful lack of access points seemed larger than my maps or my previous experience could suggest. I would catch small browns on an Elk Hair Caddis as I worked my way past the Seven-Mile Pool and its primitive camping site. I would ease my walk as the gradient lessened and October leaves began to fall throughout the Devil's Den area of cliffs. I would see large browns spawning in places like the Old Hickory Pool, taking cover quickly as I crept along at a heron's pace. Ultimately, Slate Run would show me its curves and straightened alleys, its depths and shallows, its fish and its forested slopes.

Its flow would be forever within me, as it was here and now at the Manor Falls Pool in March. This pool is probably the most popular and most heavily fished location on the run. It's a big pool with an unknown depth; I've heard estimations of up to 20 feet deep. Large trout have come from the pool; timber rattlesnakes have slithered down from the mountain to drink from its sides; young campers have enjoyed leaping into it from the rocks above.

Today I didn't fish it hard, just a few casts with a pair of weighted nymphs, with a vision of a warmer day, the upstream walk continuing.

6

"...Mayfly hatches on Slate Run include Blue Quills, Quill Gordons, Hendricksons, March Browns, Green Drakes, Blue-winged Olives, Sulphurs, Cahills, and Slate Drakes. A variety of caddis hatch prolifically throughout the warmer months. Stoneflies are important as well. During the summer, terrestrial fishing can be very good. A Black Ant, beetle imitation, and a Green Weenie (a local favorite) are effective patterns.

It is best to wear drab or camouflage clothing when you fish Slate Run. If you use a wading staff, a rubber cap on the bottom is recommended to muffle the noise produced by metal. Stalk your quarry like a heron and use an upstream approach. Walk slowly and minimize your profile and your shadow on the stream. Cast to the nearest trout first before wading to the head of a pool. The low, clear water requires stealth and the use of long, light leaders. Enjoy your catch but, unlike that premier fisher, the heron, give your trout a quick release.

Slate Run is a wild trout stream. The fish here are not the cookie-cutter stocked trout found in many other streams and rivers. The fish rely on instincts to evade predators such as otters, herons, and human beings. You may not catch as many fish on Slate as you might on some heavily stocked waters, but these trout are beautiful and born here in the Pennsylvania mountains...."

Micro-Flyfishing

1

When I speak of micro-flyfishing I am not referring to the fashionable Tenkara style of fishing in America. Tenkara is an ancient Japanese form of fishing with a long rod, fly and line that has recently become quite popular in the States. I have not yet pursued it, but I'm sure it's fun and quite satisfying to those who have adopted this simplified style of angling with collapsible rod and line. I think I'm stuck forever, though, in my Western angling ways, immersed blissfully in the expanding universe of here and now. I find myself thinking, sure, I *could* go simpler with Tenkara, but wouldn't that be inflating my trout concerns a little too much, or getting in a little over my head?

So, what do I mean by micro-fishing with a fly? I'm inferring that an angler can minimize his or her presence on the stream and grow a little smaller and humbler in the arms of wild nature. It's a simple act, really, and I suspect that many anglers do this sort of thing without making a conscious effort at it. Micro-flyfishing, though, seems unlike any other aspect of the game in that you wade into the fish's world and then look out at your own place with a new perspective.

Small trout streams range in size from step-across to pools that sometimes measure up to 30 feet in width. Fishing these minimal flows can be especially stimulating in the spring or autumn when the water levels are higher and the temperatures are good for fish activity. Brooks and streamlets tend to have less in the way of insect hatches or reliable groceries than their larger counterparts, so their trout will often feed on whatever comes along. These fish cannot afford to be choosy in their eating habits. The fly-fisher would do well to be prepared with attractor patterns like the Royal Wulff or Adams in the warmer months, along with terrestrial patterns like the Ant or Black Beetle, and with bead-head nymphs and small streamers in the cooler seasons.

Just because the trout of small streams will be less selective in their choice of fly doesn't mean the angler should forget about a careful strategy for approaching the water. These are wild fish and they need to be extremely wary to survive. The angler would do well to stalk as cautiously as possible—the fly rod is an instrument not unlike a heron's eye and beak.

I'll typically approach these small streams with a fly rod as short as a 5'9" two-weight or as large as a 7-foot four-weight. I use a floating line with attached leader that is tapered to about a 5X tippet and that measures slightly shorter than the rod. You'll often do a lot of climbing, dodging, crawling, and cursing on these streams, but you're in the trout's world now, so you don't want to be overburdened with equipment. No doubt it's a place for the Tenkara angler, too. Casting lightly here is part of the attraction in fishing small.

Often, using less of everything on these streams is tantamount to success. Use less rod, less line and less leader than on larger waters. In the beautiful, constricted worlds of the small wild trout, you'll employ less power and casting distance. If the artificial fly has a barbless hook, it's easy to make a quick release of the fish that's seldom injurious. The fish you catch will be mostly small, usually colorful, and always valuable to the stream and landscape. In my humble opinion, each captured trout should be returned unharmed to its original haunts. I don't have a problem with campers who want a tasty meal fried from a legal catch, if they know the stream is healthy enough to offer a sacrificial few.

2

In micro-flyfishing you'll involve yourself with a constantly changing approach to the stream. As you hunt for likely looking cover, try to stalk along the bank as much as possible and avoid the temptation to wade. Streamwalking sends shock waves to the quarry all too readily. Since trout face the current and can see in all directions but behind, it's preferable to walk upstream along the bank or on the water's edge rather than fishing down. Keeping out of view, you can often approach to a point nearly above the fish.

Walking from one piece of water to the next, you'll probably need to review your strategy or adopt a new one. You could have a tiny pool in front of you one moment and then, in the next, you'll be looking at an undercut bank or a monstrous tangle of branches. For each new location, figure on a strategy that minimizes the risk of spooking the trout. Wild fish are always watchful to avoid the spear or the paw of predators, and with one wrong move on your part they are gone.

Learn to recognize a trout's protective shelter, which could be a deep hole, undercut, boulder, log, or other protuberance. A trout's small house will always have a door from which it can dart for a morsel of arriving food. A good house is one that allows the best security while minimizing the risk in grabbing food. Keeping this in mind, you'll optimize your chances of success.

I use several different mini-casts while fishing the small stream. The first one is seldom needed: the fly-fisherman's forward/backward cast. In the wild trout's tiny world, whether it be on a meadow brook or on a wooded mountain stream, you'll rarely have the chance to do the far-and-fine. The second cast that I employ here is the underhand swing. When you've worked yourself into a ridiculous position surrounded by a welter of possible snags and overhangs, a cautious underhand swing may be your only option for that hungry-looking trout. You simply swing your shortened line and leader to a point ahead of the fish and pray that the gods are on your side.

A third feed, the roll cast, is probably the one I use most often in the tight realm of the brook. With a length of line on the water in front of me, I raise the rod and line. With a forward snap of the casting arm, the wrist and the rod propel the line to another choice location. Finally, there's a fourth cast to consider while inside restrictive areas of the stream: It's the bow-and-arrow, or the bow, cast. This one is a little tricky to learn, but once you've got it there's a lot of good holding water that will open for you, water that's untouchable with any other type of cast. I use it on almost every small stream outing.

The bow cast starts from a crouch position, often on one or both knees. Facing the target area, grasp the barbless hook with two fingers of your casting hand. With the fingers of your opposite hand, control the fly line at a point along the rod from which you'll want the line to carry forward. Pull back the fly and leader so that the rod flexes upward toward the forward-cast position. Aiming at a target upstream of the trout's location (real or imagined), carefully release the fly and line from your fingers. Try to keep the casts short and accurate, and keep the best part of your line and leader off the water as the fly drifts closer to your position.

When a fish rises or you see a flash of motion underwater, set the hook. Apply pressure on the fish by holding the line tightly against the rod handle and by stripping in excess line. Occasionally you may need to use side-arm pressure on a larger fish to keep it away from obstacles like roots and logs.

3

The joy and satisfaction to be found in small stream fishing is dependent on the energy you put into it. There's nothing mystical in the process. Small streams are always a challenge to fish, but that's part of their appeal, and any challenge that is met on the water is worth the time and energy involved.

You'll probably find solitude and beauty on the stream. Your labors in the angling microcosm will unveil a whole new sense of exploration and adventure.

Your pursuit of small native trout, or of wild fishes in general, will be looked upon as "fun." Other people won't be viewing you as having fun because, most likely, you'll be alone, or in enough seclusion that a fishing partner won't see you land that rare big fish, the one that puts a grin on your face and makes an indelible impression on your memory bank.

In micro-flyfishing you adapt your expectations to meet the small and beautiful. As you adapt and change those expectations from the usual to the extraordinary, as you catch and release six or seven-inch native trout with micro-tackle, you'll begin to see the silken, multi-hued skins of fish as a form of living poetry, a visual connection to an all-encompassing realm. They're like the textures and aromas of the varied plants and animals surrounding you on the stream.

As you bore deeply into the world of small stream trout, the wildness that surrounds you keeps the body tuned and balanced. When a nine or a 10-inch trout rises from a plunge-pool of a five-foot waterfall, you've hooked a relative monster. When you hook a rare 17-inch brown in such a pool (or from another totally surprising site), the micro-world is suddenly massive, and you know you'll be quiet about this catch, knowing that even if you told your friends, they'd probably scratch their heads and figure that you've got some ego issues to be settled.

You've discovered a special place that you can call your own. No, you haven't escaped from the reality of an overcrowded earth, but very few others have ventured this far from the road or path, and that, alone, feels unusually fine.

4

I recently saw a muscle car with a message on the back that read, "Hang on, I feel like taking a chance!" That's how I was feeling as I prepared for tackling two streams in two days, each one with a mile of water that I hoped to cover. A double-haul cast of fly line isn't necessary on this kind of stream, but to double-haul my outings would be good for mental health.

On what I call the "Miracle Mile" of a trout stream close to home, I was on skinny water in September eager to try a newly tied Grouse and Flash, a soft-hackle fly, a pattern based on the traditional Partridge and Orange. I liked the contrast between the dark grouse fibers and the pearly Mylar tinsel that seemed to be like the difference between fishing on a small stream on a day with rain and storm predictions and casting in a river on a clear day with plenty of fish and anglers. I enjoyed the fishing on a tight stream with solitude and dark clouds overhead, but by the time that the rain rolled in and the wind kicked up, the Grouse and Flash pattern still had not produced.

The next day I was driving into northern Pennsylvania to fish the second stream, a favorite run in low water conditions. I was passing pipelines, gas rigs, trucks and more trucks in a world that seemed to be industrializing quickly as our globe was heating up and burning and flooding. Sure, it looked like money, but not the kind of money that I liked to earn. And I felt like a hypocrite, driving a gas-powered vehicle while heading toward a great escape, complaining of an industry's chokehold on these beautiful lands and waters. I had my distractions but I tried not to let them excuse me from personal responsibilities and thoughts about my place in the world of man and nature. I tried to hold to this dual-screen image of life until I found my drab, cool canyon and its little stream. There I discovered a balance of mountains and valleys, of freedom and energy use, and there I hoped to be forgiven my own errors while pursuing a sort of spiritual path upstream.

This is where I'd do my micro-fishing for a day, starting off by casting a bead-head Prince. This is where I'd take my chances like the driver of a muscle car. And this is where I'd end a day of searching for trout, of catching and releasing wild fish in a small mountain stream, like ripples in a pool becalmed by autumn light.

Autumn Journal

1

A friend of mine from Wellsville, New York on the upper Genesee River was dealing with a major health issue, and I was glad to see that a benefit was being staged for him at a local VFW site. This friend was a well-known soft-hackle fly tier, co-founder of our local TU chapter, and an artist who has championed the use of wingless wet flies and the fishing arts of James Leisenring and Vern Hidy. It was good to mingle with associates and family of the artist and with community members ready to support my friend and to wish him the best. There were plenty of items to be raffled at the benefit dinner and Chinese auction, and my wife held the lucky ticket for a set of artificial-fly prints photographed by Lance Hidy, a renowned graphic designer and professor who also happens to be a son of the late author and fly-fisher, Vern Hidy.

The mounted prints were frame-able, my ticket to further research about wingless wet flies and their history going back to the origins of British fly-fishing in the northern parts of England. As a life-long student of the vast outdoors and of our ways of finding peace and satisfaction there, I was ready to learn more.

My late friend from Wellsville was truly versed in the subject of soft-hackle flies and "flimphs" (a Hidy term for a blend of nymph and wet fly), and his three prints of graphic art in my possession were a ticket into a new realm of angling tradition and cold-water basics, not to mention the warm relations of my friend's community and family ties. Again, an old environmental truth appeared as if on a giant screen inside my head: Cold clean water is connected to everything else in the natural world and the well-being of our human lives.

2

Lately I've been thinking of some anchor holds in this crazy life of mine. The first thing that came to mind is not the most significant anchor hold, but it's a hefty one, in my opinion:

Fly-fishing is my anchor hold in a world gone mad. Fly-fishing is an anchor hold when humankind departs from nature. Fly-fishing is my anchor hold in a vast river of the earth. Fly-fishing is an anchor hold in the lively waters of my home.

Poetry and writing help maintain an even keel. Friends and family, of course. Without them I'd be cut adrift in the solitude of stormy oceans.

Home, this place in the country where I've lived by choice for more than 35 years. Home, where now the autumn colors fade with each new burst of rain, as the specter of an oncoming winter looms behind each hill and new horizon.

The World Series in a time of numbing political campaign overkill. "Giants/Tigers vs. Clinton/Trump."

Baseball! *Rivertop Rambles*, the photo/essay blog that I've maintained for years. A poem called "One Year," from my first collection of poetry, *Talking to the Owls*, (1984):

The rough-legged hawk/ returns down the ridges from/ the north. A single leaf cuts/ loosely through west wind/ as golden birches grapple/ blue sky. Everything/ hurries somewhere even/ as we stop & build this rest. / A woodpecker stalks the barn wall. Crowns of red pine hold October's/ waning moon, the way myriad/ events contain the moment, / life diminishing as it grows....

Walking through the woods out back I found raw evidence of change in the trees. A large maple, dead but standing when I first saw it many years ago, had finally toppled over. Each time that I'd seen the rotted but stately form throughout the years I wondered when it would happen, when this home for ants and woodpeckers and red squirrels would collapse into its final rest on the duff. At last I saw it—three sprawling, rotted logs that had once been a thriving oxygen producer. Since no one else had lived with this tree as a dead and standing form, no one else would have noticed its passing, a small life gone on a hill with a thousand autumn changes.

In a season of excessive media noise, political campaigning, advertising lies, and warfare, not to mention economic and psychological stresses, I imagined that the old tree fell inside its woodlot with a resounding *krak!* It must have been a welcome noise, an anchor hold, even though no two-legged being was around to hear it. The hills and mountains were advancing into autumn and, ultimately, their leafless winter forms. They were so old, they made a veteran streamwalker feel like new.

3

I moved on to a small trout stream and fished with permission on a lovely stretch of private water. A mink swam ahead of me while hunting fish. I was glad I didn't have to compete. Like a mink, I often fish alone, enjoying the solitude and feel of wildness, although I also like to fish with a partner when I'm able, sharing the experience and the kick of camaraderie. Mostly I fish alone because compatible partners are difficult to come by, often living too far away to meet with on a regular basis. Many of the anglers I know are just not as obsessed, or crazy, about fly-fishing, nor are they as willing to creep, crawl and curse their way through the jungles of growth often found on eastern brook trout waters.

I finished my day where a spring brook wends its way into the larger stream. A high sandy bank along the creek supports many trees planted by our chapter of Trout Unlimited. I tied on a dry fly pattern known as "Purple Haze." This Adams variant tied in the parachute style was one of several Hazes that I purchased in Montana... Purple Haze... I made a delicate cast to a deep riffle and thought of Jimi Hendrix, watching the fly parachute to its designated spot on the water and waiting for a flourish equal to a fine distortion of musical phrase. A sizeable brown trout chased the drifting fly and seized it. The fish shot downstream and spit out the Haze before I knew what was happening... Stone free... I pulled in the line, the leader and the fly, empty as the hour, buoyant as the creek.

As I said, I often fish alone, but I also love companionship at times. One day I was casting in upstate New York's Fall Creek, watching the broad autumnal stream pour beneath a great willow tree and sensing that time, the multiple years that I'd pursued salmon with a fly, was like a tumbling river. I was mid-stream near a bridge and it was difficult to sight-fish for the landlockeds and the browns where they had come to rest, although occasionally I had glimpses of the mobile, leaden-colored ghosts.

"He's lying under the tree, under that big purple fly there on the branch." I looked at a gaudy streamer sacrificed to the great pursuit of trout and salmon. A fly-fisher standing on the bridge would help me out. "Whoa, it's a large salmon!" he exclaimed.

Lacking his bird's-eye vantage point, I cast dutifully toward the spot he indicated. "Go another foot closer to the bank." My next cast was on the mark; the Woolly Bugger brushed a nose but, as I heard it from my guide on the bridge, the salmon darted away.

I tried casting Egg flies, stoneflies, Egg-sucking Leeches, and even a Gray Ghost streamer, but the big ones were street-wise, river-wise, and lake-wise, too, and wouldn't have any of it that day. But Fall Creek had been good to me in the past; I'd wrestled with plenty of landlocked salmon and brown trout in the 20 to 28-inch range while fishing there, and I couldn't complain. As my angling friend departed from the bridge, he wished me good luck then said, "And if you don't have any luck, enjoy your beer!" I told him thanks; I'd already been looking forward to a bottle.

4

Autumn on the upper Allegheny River. Time for an inspection of the Woolly Bugger and the Egg fly. The famous Bugger was invented by the late Russ Blessing, a Pennsylvania angler who fished Slate and Cedar Run. As for the Egg, or Glo-Bug, it's a pattern with a sense of humor. The Egg seems to ask if it's really an artificial "fly" or not. As in, which came first, the Chicken-Hackled Dun Fly or the Egg? I used to be reluctant to cast the bright orange globule of compressed fibers because it didn't seem to have the dignity of, let's say, a Gold-ribbed Hare's Ear or a Royal Wulff. To use it seemed akin to casting a rubber worm or an artificial hatchery pellet, and the damn thing even seemed to question one's morality as an angler. Wasn't the Egg an imitation of life at its *conception*, a taboo subject in a sport like this?

I got over that eventually. Almost. Through the years, I've fished the Egg innumerable times in early spring or autumn while pursuing salmon, steelhead or upland trout. Yet even today, on the Allegheny where only artificial flies and lures can be legally cast, I probably paused a moment or two to ask myself again, is it okay to use this thing? This twist of neon yarn, this bright star of creation trimmed for the hook, this tiny ball of stuff that triggers an avalanche of response in a trout…

When the Egg struck shallow water, I saw a trout shoot upstream for 10 feet or more, only to stop and reconsider. Then, as the Egg bounced slowly on another drift along the river bottom, the trout resigned itself to instinct and bit on the orange. Minutes later, another rainbow struck from deeper water, in a seam of fast and slower currents. The rainbow, in all 17 inches of cold water fury, put a full flex in my bloodstream and the bamboo fibers as it leapt from the water and circled through the river pool. As I walked back to the car I had to reconsider the effectiveness of an Egg: a simple construct, an archetypal piece of fluff, and *more*.

5

A dozen cars were parked at the bridge where I typically gain access to the Lake Ontario tributary, more than I usually note when pulling up for a day of autumn fishing. Those cars meant two things: there would be a lot of fishing pressure near the bridge (though miles of open water might be found between it and the next access point), and… the big trout must be coming up for the spawn.

The creek was flowing high and colored, and the morning sun was disappearing as the rain clouds drifted in again. My primary interest that day was finding brown trout on a spawning mission. In the past, I had taken and released some beautiful large trout in this location, but in recent years those encounters had been sparse.

Once I got past the "Pittsburgh 8," a group of fly-fishing friends from Pennsylvania, I found my open water. The pools and riffles were deep and lively. At first the fish were difficult to distinguish in the darkened water, but then their size and movements gave them away.

Around noon the rain began in earnest, lightly at first and then more steadily. Protected by a rain jacket, I felt comfortable. The big surprise for me was that the chinook and the coho salmon runs were still in progress. In fact, the late arrivals, green and full of locomotive heat, were still streaming in from the lake.

At their redds, the salmon were more aggressive toward an artificial fly than they were on my previous visit, and my hook-ups were frequent. One fair-hooked salmon struggled like a defeated heavyweight boxer till I finally slid it to the bank and taped its length at 41 inches.

With only an hour or two before I needed to depart, I still hadn't landed a brown, although I knew they were checking in. A few other guys were hauling out the trout, and it looked as though more fish were arriving as the afternoon wore on. I'd been trying several favorite fly patterns, but decided to continue with the salmon favorite of the day, a Woolly Bugger with a chartreuse head.

In deep riffles near the bank, I saw what looked to be another resting chinook. Standing upstream of the fish, I passed the streamer out in front and felt the take. A large brown was on the line, a full-bodied female that I quickly photographed and measured at 26 inches before guiding it back into the flow. Satisfied, I prepared to leave, but while approaching the bridge, I came to another pause.

The fish I saw and made a cast to wasn't the fish that struck. A male brown came out of nowhere, from the murky depths behind or off to the side of my original target here. I caught a glimpse of color like Halloween orange, and felt a weight and a thrashing struggle uncommon while fishing for browns.

The trout, a record brown for me, was a 30-inch male with a massive kype. Its photos, taken in the rain, do not do justice for the fish. If I was friendly with a taxidermist, I might have considered taking this excellent brown trout to the wall but, instead, I worked it back to the safety of the pool.

It was time to go. I had come to the creek in search of unusual browns and, by route of a surprising salmon run, had finally found them. No doubt the browns, in addition to spawning, were feeding heavily on salmon eggs.

6

The sensation was a little spooky. I was fishing with friends on northern New York's Salmon River, and no one was catching anything, not the hardware angler on the bank, not the guys out wading with a fly rod, nor the numerous client/guide combinations drifting by in boats. The chinooks had long expired and were little more than ghostly carcasses wavering on the river bottom, but the big browns and the steelhead should've been more visible despite the dark and turbulent water, and there should have been hook-ups left and right. There was next to nothing, despite our best attempts.

The sky was making its first reference to distant Hurricane Sandy, but the air was comfortable and we were determined to make the most of it. After about seven hours of desperately flogging the river with our fly lines, everybody quit.

In retrospect, it seems logical to blame the poor fishing on a crash of barometric pressure signaling the imminent blend of Sandy with a couple of cold fronts moving in from the west and north, but who's to say we just weren't cutting it as steelhead anglers? Sure, the coming "super-storm" would be one of the largest to whack America in recent times, but I like to think there were at least a few wayward spawners in the Salmon willing to boost our egos while tugging at our fishing lines.

I remember standing thigh-deep in the river when I got a mid-morning call. Not the kind where you've got to stumble toward the bank and divest yourself of angling attire, but a call with a ring tone emanating from a pants pocket. My flip-top "dumb phone" had no Caller Identification, so when I finally got the phone in hand, I had no idea who was trying to reach me. The voice told me it wasn't my wife. It had the growl and slur of some guy with a vicious hangover.

"Ay! What're ya doin?"

"Well, right now I'm drifting a Woolly Bugger in the river."

"Wha'? Oh... Ah'm sorry; I tried callin' 607-538-0624."

"No problem. I just wish you were a big old steelhead with some good advice 'cause I'm not catching *anything*!"

Back at home I found an email from my good friend George in London. He had just read my latest Autumn Journal post on *Rivertop Rambles* while under the influence of listening to Brian Eno's ambient album, *On Land*. That's interesting, I thought. On land. A message from across the big blue pond. I'd always been fond of that album and the deep mysterious environment it evoked through sonic art. The night before, as Hurricane Sandy raged across the New York landscape, I tried to sympathize with all the victims of the storm, especially to the east where the Big One really slammed the coastal towns, and I also listened to some music.

Again, I listened to *On Land*, especially to the piece called "Unfamiliar Wind." I was lifted out of Sandy to a quiet place of utter solitude, replete with a tropic beauty far beyond my comprehension. I needn't have gone, of course; I could've taken up with the darker wind outside my door, but I felt like answering a different call.

A Creek with Almost Everything

1

After a cold front brought some rain to northern Pennsylvania, I visited lower Cross Fork Creek for the first time in several years. I parked at the dead-end road where a snowmobile bridge crosses the flow just upstream of its confluence with Kettle Creek. The stream was low and a bit off-color. For the first half mile or so of this catch-and-release water, fishing wasn't worth the effort. There was little structure, or life-supporting habitat for trout, in the stream – much less than I remembered from before.

But Cross Fork is a scenic trout stream, one of the better wild trout fisheries in the region, and this little sister of Kettle Creek is a pleasure to traverse even when there's a drought on the land. I strolled along with a seven-foot fly rod in my clutches, hopeful that better water would be located just around the bend.

In fact, the stream *was* better just around the bend; it seemed to improve with each new spring and tributary I encountered on the upstream walk. It even had a white pine "shit'er," or outhouse, on its greeny south bank. This cool, natural structure had been renovated since my previous passage here, but it still had a perfect view of the water for an angler in need. The crapper functions as a wild convenience, indeed, replete with a plastic case to shield the toilet paper. I couldn't imagine a finer throne in all of Potter County.

You've got to be an angling saint or a nature-loving sage to be unconcerned with finding fish, and I was certainly no saint or enlightened philosopher at Cross Fork Creek. I looked for trout in this special regulation water (catch-and-release) and finally got a hook-up where the stream poured by an undercut bank. I was ready to abandon the tandem wet flies I'd been using (Green Weenie and Partridge-and-Orange) when an unseen fish shot into the current and absconded with my tippet and two flies.

Encouraged, I proceeded to a large pool where I saw several rise formations at the surface. Switching to a dry Black Ant I made a long cast and observed a rise coming laterally from yards away. I struck too soon and felt the hook strafe a lip. Several casts later I had another hook-up with a large brown, all too brief. I inched closer to the head of a pool. I finally got a brown trout on the line and it came to hand, my only catch for the morning. That was it, enough, though miles of wild trout waters beckoned from the hills above.

This creek even has its own village, with two restaurant/taverns or, as I call them, "fishing bars." The village is close, but not too close, to the stream. On my rating scale of 1 to 5 Beers, I rated Jack's Bar (not its real name) as a "1 Beer" watering hole that day. The beer selections were average; the ambience was good, but the racist patron chatter was too much for me to stomach (typically I enjoy blue-collar conversations while imbibing cold beverages but I draw the line at bullshit that is obviously hurtful).

More enjoyable was Darlene's Place (again not its real name), the saloon across the street where the folks were friendly, the refreshments good, and the ambience (including a big stuffed bobcat) comfortable. I particularly enjoyed listening to an elderly, bearded guy who carves iconic images out of rock and bone, especially from antlers and… "raccoon dick." I gave the place a 3 Beer rating on my fish-bar scale.

The creek not only has its own two bars, it even has another stream to fish in! It has Kettle Creek, a larger water, into which it flows near Cross Fork village. I decided to sample the Kettle's catch-and-release section with a longer, eight-foot rod that I had brought along for the occasion.

The Kettle had a decent 62-degree temperature but its flow was minimal. The trout weren't moving. I released a smallmouth bass and several chubs. After Cross Fork Creek, the Kettle proved anticlimactic this day, but so what. A trout stream isn't made solely for a fisherman's delight.

2

My subject isn't necessarily Cross Fork Creek; it's the kind of place you find near home, but only after years of trial and error. My subject is the kind of place you head to for a day of solitude and beauty. You might go there for the birds and wildflowers, for a hike or an easy ramble, for a hunt that only you can define. You might go there to inspect a population of native trout.

You might go there to relax or to forget what's better left forgotten. You might go there to remember that the world is larger than it was while you were working. You might go there to remind yourself that people aren't the center of creation.

There are trout and orioles and multiflora roses in June. Sometimes there's a good friend with you, one who loves the game as much as you do, one who even claims to understand what it is you're looking for.

You might go there to roughen up your edges, to enhance the texture of your time on earth. And you know that whatever it is, there's wildness in the mix.

If you're like me, you might go there because you're insufferable on occasion, perhaps a pain in the ass to others who might need some time to themselves. You might go there because it's good for society (as if you really cared), which gets you out of the store and office for a while.

You might go there to find another green world—a place to renew your hope for all mankind. If you do that, my advice would be to stay open-minded. Nature doesn't care to work with us or to conform its ways to fit our personal needs. Be prepared for small surprises and the need for adaptation.

You might go there for the highlight of your week, but it's possible that the fish won't bite. The bugs and heat and high humidity could be an unexpected headache. And that's just part of the fun you'll have.

You might go there for a grand finale of some sort. On this trip (not necessarily to Cross Fork Creek), I stopped for a beer at the Old Tannery Saloon. The place was quiet, unlike a neighboring bar where the parking lot was filled with high school grads and bikers and summer folk. The grimy walls were covered with everything from a hanging bear trap to a photo of 20 topless ladies smiling on a yacht.

It was my kind of bar. In fact, an older couple (probably in their 70s) got up from their stools to pay for their bill. The man asked, "How was the fly-fishing today?"

"Oh… It was good," I answered, surprised that anyone had noticed my fishing shirt and hat in the dim light of the old saloon.

"What were you using?" The gentleman pulled his tipsy wife closer to his side.

"Dry flies. The fish were rising, especially on the East Fork."

Then the wife had a question: "And what pattern were you using?"

"Blue-winged Olive. It was that kind of weather. Dark and showery."

The man and woman nodded vigorously, as if the pattern was the most reasonable response in the world. With a wave of the hand, they were out the door, and I finished off my Straub.

I gave the Old Tannery a 4 Beer rating on my 1 to 5 fish-bar scale. Like Cross Fork Creek, itself, the bar had almost everything.

3

All week long I'd been looking for Mr. Hendrickson, my personification of the great Eastern mayfly hatch. Because of the cold wet spring, this first of the big mayfly hatches in the region was expected to be later than usual, but it could happen any day that Mr. Hendrickson saw fit.

The artificial pattern for this fly was first created by the Catskill tier, Roy Steenrod, around 1920, for a fishing customer named Hendrickson. The mayfly, *Ephemera subvaria*, is heralded by Eastern anglers as a key player in the new dry fly season, the nymphs emerging from the depths of a stream to unfold their wings on the surface and dry them long enough to stir a feeding frenzy in the trout.

The adult insects have smoky blue wings. The female has a light pink body, and the male has a darker, reddish cast. The females tend to hatch from one section of a stream, a riffle perhaps, and the males tend to hatch from another. Mr. Hendrickson, my personification of this complex critter, is an interesting fellow who, in my estimation, contains both male and female parts.

About a week ago, I was well inside the woods and looking for Hendrickson duns when I heard a rustle downstream. I saw a gray-haired angler who, approaching the pool that I was sampling, proved to be a female, astonishingly enough.

I love it that more and more women are taking to the field these days, but I rarely see one fishing solo, that is, without a male partner nearby. This angler, wearing camouflage and plastic, sauntered in and asked what I was using for bait. I showed her my tandem nymphs. "Oh, flies," she said. "I should try them sometime, but I *really* like my nightcrawlers."

With that comment, the lady swung her weighted crawler to a root wad in my pool, and continued: "Let's see if there's a trout hiding under there." Luckily, no trout responded. She was not Mr. Hendrickson, I acknowledged confidently. Reeling in my line, I excused myself and slunk away.

On the weekend, I was privileged to fish a neighboring stream, about a mile of private water on one of the best freestone creeks in Pennsylvania. I was looking for a 3 o'clock hatch of Hendricksons when I chanced to meet another fly-fisherman coming my way. We paused to chat about the weather, of how we humans love a bright spring day whereas the trout probably have a different take on the value of the sun. We commented on each other's bamboo rod, on the maker of the sticks, on how many pieces each contained and what their lengths were. When bamboo-wielding anglers suddenly meet out of nowhere on a peaceful stream, I dare say the scene is not unlike two curious dogs meeting for the first time and sniffing tails.

I commented on the prospect of a Hendrickson hatch, and the other fellow said that it could happen. "I start looking for them when the shadbush blossoms," he said. A variety of blooms were on the forest and the streambanks. I looked at this guy and knew him to be older than myself (believe it or not), and almost bursting with life experience. I wondered if he was Hendrickson, himself.

The next day I was out on the same northern Pennsylvania stream, and now the sky was overcast. Wonderful, I thought. Clouds, along with the prospect of rain, might spur some insect hatches! I began by casting a pair of wets, but as mid-afternoon arrived and the first few Hendrickson duns appeared on the surface, I switched to a dry fly.

Ten minutes later the rain began to lightly fall. The temperature was dropping. I saw a splash on quiet water near a riffle, and I knew that surface feeding had begun. A specimen of Roy Steenrod's mayfly, in living color, landed on my wrist and perched there in the stiffening breeze. Before a gust of wind blew it away, and before I made a roll-cast to the narrow feeding lane, I made my introduction…

"Mr. Hendrickson, I presume."

4

Any stream that's equipped with "almost everything" must surely be well-stocked with "nymphs" in all their manifestations.

Most fly-fishermen and budding entomologists are aware of nymphs, the immature stage of numerous insects that develop in the water. Many anglers fly-fish with an artificial nymph, often allowing their imitative lure to drift along the current of a stream or river at some level well below the surface.

Less well-known is the fact that nymphs were female spirits representing the various aspects of sacred nature. The ancient Greeks peopled every room of nature with divinities. Nymphs were feminine energies, short of the divine realm but with links to the eternal. They personified the beauty of specific places, and they often lived long lives. They persist today in the minds and bodies of some people who are close to nature, and they reluctantly force me to say the following: fly-fishing can be sexy. It usually *isn't* sexy, but it can be.

The classic nymphs most interesting to me as a fly-fisher are the Dryads, the protectors of forest locales, and the Naiads, the protector spirits of water, i.e., of springs and streams, of rivers, marshes, ponds, and lakes. What makes them attractive to me, for other than the obvious male reasons, are their characters—unlike the gods and goddesses, they are mortal, like ourselves—plus their intimate connections to a place on earth.

The Naiads are completely dependent on the body of water that they represent. If a stream such as Cross Fork Creek dries up or becomes overly stressed, the Naiad for the creek is finished. Alive and well, the classic Naiads were sex symbols, of a sort, and played the part of a seducer (often of men and demi-gods and big fellas like Zeus). Their waters were thought to have a mixture of medicinal, prophetic and inspirational powers. People who partook of these waters, drinking them or fishing in them, were said to be "captured by the nymphs."

These spirits of locales are attractive because they're personal, and thus beyond the point of general worship. We'll make no religion out of nymphing (we could leave religion to the dry fly purists, maybe). And we'll not speak of "nymphomania," leaving that to psychology majors, nor of "nymphets," as in the great *Lolita*.

All of which leads me to a recent evening on the river. I went there expecting a hatch of *Isonychia* and saw examples of the big gray mayfly on the surface, but the trout weren't rising to them, for some reason or another. After half an hour of futile casting, I was about to quit, but then decided to give the long pool one last shot with an *Isonychia* nymph.

Drifting the fly deeply through the current at the head of the pool, it was as if I had called upon the crafters of beauty there to open the door. It was as if some deity, personified, gave answer to the call. It gave me the power of poetry and the visible embodiment of something almost divine. Yes, like any fine creek with almost everything in its rambling nature, the evening river lent me the biggest brown trout of the season so far—a solid 21-inch brown that fell for a tantalizing... I want to say "Naiad," but will settle for... artificial nymph.

Self-Portrait of the Fisherman as Idler

1

I'd been fishing every day for more than a week, which is interesting, from my perspective, given the dry summer conditions in the eastern U.S., and the fact that I was holding down the fort at home while also assisting an elderly woman, my mother, each day in the final stages of her life.

It seemed that the so-called idleness of fishing helped to keep me balanced somehow. As author Robert Louis Stevenson notes in his essay "An Apology for Idlers," idleness does not consist of doing nothing, rather, of doing lots of things not recognized by the status quo. After all, my aim here is to paint a picture of the fisherman as an idler, not as a fool, or idiot.

Idleness seems at least as important as breaking your chops in industry. But some folks who labor all their lives, who work more than necessary to fulfill the basic requirements of a good life for themselves and loved ones, don't get it when they hear that a fellow can prowl along the stream each day or stand in the river of time with a fishin' pole in hand.

It's not easy being good at idleness. It's not easy being curious and investigative or imaginative while others simply amass a fortune. Hey, to each his own. We've all got bills to pay and big responsibilities to fulfill. But can't we strike a happy medium?

We do what we've got to do. I may be a writer with a job to check out the milkweed bloom or the gorgeous color on a brook trout, then to try to stimulate the interests of other people, too. There isn't much compensation for it, but writing is a labor I enjoy.

People are busy with their complicated lives, and all too many that I know show little interest in understanding the world of nature. They don't seem generous enough to grasp this notion of "idleness." There's too little wonder or magic in their lives. A true idler, says Stevenson, won't neglect the intricacy of his or her own being that is balanced with the world.

Okay, but let's look at this thing called nature that surrounds us when we step outdoors. The world seems unimaginably vast and careless of the singular life, of you or me. If that's the case, why should any of us see ourselves as important entities within it, as candle holders to the universe?

I don't know if "important" is the right qualifier when considering the human self, but I would say that we're important, or hold a candle to our lives, when we view ourselves as small and humble. As the poet William Blake once wrote, "If the doors of perception were cleansed, everything would appear to man as it is, *infinite.*" Indeed, if we could see beyond the small world of our human interactions, how could we then escape a different view of our existence?

As a budding psychology and education major in 1970, I read Blake's comment in *The Doors of Perception* by Aldous Huxley, a book that profoundly influenced my new "career" as hippie idler, poet, and trout bum wannabe. I also like the fact that the well-known L.A. rock band took its name from the Blakean phrase and title of a book.

Idleness, filled with poetry and labor of the soul, is an honorable vocation, whether we fish or sail or pitch a ball, whether we read a good book on a porch or in a hammock, or do most anything for relaxation (except watch television or playing golf… okay, just kidding, just kidding…).

2

Sometimes an Idler confronts his fear while fishing in the woods. To deal with his fear, or to stare it down in the hope of driving it away, the Idler might daydream or fantasize an escape. Collectively, his fears might get personified and be given the moniker, Fear of Fly-Fishing.

I had a day off from work and decided to try my hand at fishing. I hadn't foreseen an allergy problem occurring, or the wet humid weather, or the full moon, or the promise of heightened solar flares. I didn't know it was Friday the 13th, either.

En route to the headwaters, I realized I'd forgotten my camera that was needed for photographs to be included in a blog post I was writing. No big deal. Hell, prior to six or seven years before, I seldom had a camera on the stream and, during my best fly-fishing year ever, 2004, all I had were a few disposables. I survived. Somehow.

Things weren't going well, and I began to visualize Fear of Fly-Fishing. I watched him closely as he decided to leave his landing net in the car. He reasoned that not having it along might ensure himself of tangling with a big fish on the stream and maybe even catching it. Through reverse psychology, he figured that to walk off half-prepared, at best, might lead to something interesting here.

From the small bridge that divides the stocked fish waters from the upstream wild trout stretches, he saw significant ripples moving through the tranquil river. At first, he thought that ducks were paddling off upon detecting his arrival. But no, the rippling came from sizeable trout that swam left and right, chasing emergent insects just below the surface of the water.

Undaunted by signs, Fear of Fly-Fishing began to cast a large caddis nymph from a high bank over the pool and saw a fish come up to take it. He slid down to the level of the river hole. The trout fought him like a solar flare in the hands of an ancient god. The big rainbow got away, and he imagined that it would have filled the net he didn't bring along. If he'd had a camera with him, the trout he didn't land would've looked fantastically distorted like the fish porn that's at home in those "Me & Joe" sporting blogs and magazine articles.

When it seems that time slips away too quickly and the world goes cartwheeling madly toward oblivion, the psyche can do strange things in the name of "getting balanced." To keep Fear of Fly-Fishing from getting an upper hand on the casting rod, the angler might do well to call on idleness. He might remember a long walk on a beautiful stream where the fishing had the potential to keep his thoughts from getting convoluted and his meditations from sounding too judgmental.

On a steelhead stream in early March, it seemed odd to me that there were no other anglers parked at the usual pull-off where I start my angling day. In likelihood, an absence of fishermen here meant that there were few, if any, migratory rainbows in the creek. For whatever reason, the steelhead fishing would continue to be slow, but I was off on a straight-line hike in search of one or two trout that may have slipped upstream overnight.

If I was lucky, I might avoid running into Fear of Fly-Fishing on this venture. It was still early in the season and the water temperature was cold, but I was heartened by the promise that the sun would appear and that these tributary waters might even lure fresh steelhead from the river.

I would hike and fish for two miles on the lonely creek before entering a deep gorge where the gravel beds called to the spawning fish before their journeys ended at a plunge-pool of a waterfall. I trudged along the snow-filled banks and occasionally crossed the stream's 30 to 40-foot width.

If I did encounter Fear of Fly-Fishing, it would be where chandeliers of ice were melting from the heights of the shadowed gorge. It was possible that he'd appear there in all his ugly glory. I didn't know what to expect from him in March, but during the warmer months he looked a lot like me, or else he was suited up in thunderstorms, poison ivy, rattlesnakes and ticks. He'd be spouting off about mother bears with cubs, of lying broken-legged at the bottom of cliffs, stuff like that. Ordinarily I ignored his lame remarks and terrible casting practices, while also trying to give him due respect. He wasn't a simple guy, but here I mostly forgot about him as I studied the dark, clay-colored stream for signs of life.

Finally, inside the cold gorge not far from the waterfall, I noticed something different about the creek. There was liveliness in the flow, a squiggly line or two reflecting from the current and raising me above my idle hopes. Those lines may have been reflections of a weed or a stick or some underwater stone but, then again, they may have been given by a fish.

My streamer drifted repeatedly through deep riffles where the lines had emanated and, at last, a fish made a pass at the lure and started running. The 8-weight rod got bent respectably but then subdued the battling steelhead—a light-colored female slightly smaller than the average runner for this creek. Close to two-feet long, the sleek and silvery rainbow was very much alive. I quickly took a photograph then slid her back to her temporary domain with several forward and backward motions.

Launching from my knees submerged in the stony edges of the creek, I glanced to the woods and saw Him there, Fear of Fly-Fishing, lurching off like an apprehended poacher embarrassed to be seen. He was dressed in camouflage, and I wondered if he had been trying for a close approach, maybe to surprise me and to rip the fly rod from my hand.

3

I went to the stream to examine my motives for trout fishing in a hot dry month and at a time when I had plenty of non-angling responsibilities to maintain. I was fishing when most streams in the area had minimal flows and marginal water temperatures, when most of the local fly-fishers had given up for now, or were hundreds of miles away.

I had left the house at dawn and was headed for a mountain stream. I listened to blues on a college radio station, knowing its format framed my expectations. "Even a blind dog sometimes finds a bone," sang the husky-voiced blues man, as if to an angler headed upstream by himself.

Fishing with compatible others is a good thing, but when you're living on the far side of nowhere, as I do, compatible small stream addicts might live a journey or two away. Consequently, on most of my fishing ventures, I have only my own self-portrait to argue with.

The drive to the creek was beautiful. Clouds hung low in the sky. The road dead-ended at a small closed bridge. I suited up and savored the misty hour. No one was around. Not an angler, nor a critic who might have seen this outing as another attempt to shirk reality. I edged through the tall grass and entered the stream. Trico spinners undulated overhead.

The current worked its magic at my ankles and lower legs, eroding the unnecessary elements as I waded upstream. The creek was low and thin, the water temperature cool.

I entered green tunnels of shrubbery. Bees droned, and a red bird sang its late season song. I broke into an opening beyond white pine trees shading the banks. My insecurities meant nothing here. A cell phone seemed as handy as a drowned plastic bag.

Again, I found that in wildness I could turn down the noise of modern living stuck inside my head. I could feel healthy for a while. The bumblebee and vireo and riffle had distinct voices. I could even conjure a persona to help me stay focused. Yes, I lost concentration and made a sloppy cast. I looked away and saw an angler up ahead. A fisherman named Henry Thoreau.

Now, wait a minute, I thought… The author of *Walden* lived in another time and place. An independent thinker and naturalist, Thoreau is an inspiration to thousands, a therapist for a broken world. In the literary realm, I could say that the author has been an inspiration to me for more years than I care to count. I've always liked the way he led the charge against conformity, the way he chided the mass of men enduring lives of quiet desperation, and the way he specified the relevance of our places here on Earth. But to think that I saw him fishing here just upstream of where I stood in mountain water was probably delusional.

I may have been deluded but, nonetheless, it seemed important to imagine Thoreau casting into a pool above the beaver dam. I imagined him as if in a trout dream. Yeah, I simply walked up to Henry and said hello to this hero of the modern world. Surely, I was humbled and honored for the opportunity. I even imagined a complex dialogue with the author/fisherman (okay, so he was casting *live bait*— who am I to judge?).

I fish for the freedom it allows, for the feeling that self-improvement is an option anyone can have. I enjoyed standing in that morning stream with the brief illusion of a literary hero at my side. The white pines shading the eastern bank of the stream suggested the presence of a wilderness past. The burble of water was an undertone to a conversation on the virtues of simplicity. If standing there was wrong because a mortal writer like myself is not supposed to mingle with the greats (as with the gods on Olympus), so be it. But if it was wrong because some literary convention forbade the meeting, i.e., suggested that this realm of the imagination was like Posted Land and not to be trespassed on, then fuck it—I was glad for the freedom, for the opportunity of Idling there with the man.

One thing that I took from my imagined rendezvous with the writer was the cool reminder that, although I carried considerably less gear than most Complete Anglers I know, it wasn't necessary to pack a great quantity of stuff. I mean, did I really need four fly boxes today? A few spools of different-sized tippet, a clipper and a bunch of Trico flies were probably enough. Even so, a surplus of equipment wasn't the greatest barrier to freedom.

Being insensitive to the special qualities of a place is like facing a concrete wall. Being unaware of the heartbeat and rhythms of water is like wearing shackles on the soul. While fishing, the main thing is to fish well in a rare place and to feel alive, to idle in perfection, if you will.

I had the feeling that Henry was planting thoughts inside my skull. I think he saw me as another desperate soul, but one unafraid to speak. I could cast a fly and he would cast a worm, but each was equal to the other as a fisherman, if not as writers on an earthly plane. The stream was beautiful, and we probably both agreed that humans everywhere would do well to love our woods and waters while we can.

It was good to cut him from my thoughts and return to clear-headed fishing. Thoreau, wherever he angled or sat as a writer, was a busy guy. People like myself pestered him too much in our own idleness. He didn't need another intrusion from the modern world. My intention may have been good but, admittedly, I'd felt like a debutante roll-casting on a mown suburban lawn. It was time for my return to what I felt most comfortable with—the things that had the names of brook trout, muskrat, pine tree, and hawk, the many things that embraced me when I walked and fished. Like old friends in a good mood, full of understanding.

4

It was a tranquil evening on the upper Genesee, accented by the constant song of robins sketching out their territories from the sycamores along the bank. With the water temperature warmer than the air, I was glad for the fishing shirt and sweater underneath the vest. They'd help me ward off the chill that would come from leaky waders. Given the time of year, I knew this cool weather with fine angling conditions wouldn't last for long.

"Take me to the river, drop me in the water… Take me to the river… And wash me on down…." It felt good to idle with the robins that seemed to know the Al Green song, the beat of the Talking Heads' cover echoed from the riffles and leaves.

I was the only one fishing the river here, except for the great blue heron poised above the upper pool.

There was plenty of room to fish and idly meditate, to sympathize with residents of many other parts of the country currently threatened by heat and fire or flood. Knock on driftwood... This part of the northland was free right now from natural miseries but, of course, that could change at any hour. I'd better be kind to the river and its song, appreciate it, fish it, sing it, while I could.

"... Wash me down... Won't you cleanse my soul... Put my feet on the ground...." To idle far, to idle long.

As I slowly worked my way upriver, casting with a 9-foot 4-weight rod, the fish came readily to the net. A dozen of them, mostly browns along with a rainbow or two. The wind at my back was a fine assistant. It would calm down completely as the robins eased their song before the dusk closed in. The best fish of the night were a couple 15 and 16-inch browns that nabbed a soft-hackle Partridge & Orange (in tandem with a floating Caddis). Nice fish for the Genesee.

If it's true that the first songs that we humans ever sang were inspired by the sounds of flowing water and the song of birds (as some believe), I saw a connection as the day died into darkness and the spinner flies of the drake and Cahill varieties began to flutter downward to the currents... *"Washing me down ... cleansing my soul..."* And as the lyrics of a different blues song recently noted, "Even a blind dog sometimes finds a bone."

5

Alright, it's autumn, and I've taken deep breaths in a crazy political climate, trying to gain some personal balance. Fishing a small group of trout streams, old and new, has been helpful, like a pill that's taken to ease a migraine. This is one of those times when it's good to get away from a perceived madness in those who run our lives, a time to try and set things right inside one's self.

For months or maybe years, I've had a few "bucket list" streams in mind, those thin blue lines on a topographic map that have beckoned me to make a visit with a fly rod. It was time to get off my ass and introduce them to my hopes as an angler.

If mind and body were feeling unusual stress, would Fear of Fly-Fishing make an appearance on those thin blue lines? Not a chance. The world of national and political change was beyond my comprehension, and my petty concerns seemed nothing more than trivial beside them. I wanted my thoughts to be idle, and a good place for idling seemed to be on the headwaters of Pine and Kettle creeks. I went there as if to greet a mentor, an admired writer or philosopher or artist who could help me paint a picture of a happier time.

I'm glad I headed upstream. The walks, the casting of a short line with a fly rod helped to clear the muddied waters of the mind.

Walking in a wild place where humanity seems little more than another tumbling rock along the stream bed, or like the fading image of Fear of Fly-Fishing himself, helped to reinforce a tentative balance. Splendid little brook trout came to hand. The barbless hook was taken from the lip; a silent word of thanks was said; the fish returned to the stream and I moved on. Walking a thin blue line, I stalked a narrow place between realities, between good and bad, right and wrong, between a world that is strong and bright and one that dwells in darkness, fear and bile.

I thanked those little streams I fished for a two-week period when I could have been busy with a lot of non-angling activities. The truth is that the little waters called me to a higher ground. I fished on streams with names like Mill Run and Trout Run, on old familiars like Fall Creek and Hammersley Fork. I thanked them all because they looked exquisite in their changing faces, and I knew they were therapeutic for those who bothered to search them out in the hope of finding consolation.

If I was a religious man I'd pray for the continued care of these streams, the way I might wish the best for disenfranchised people everywhere. When I'm feeling disgust or anger with the status quo of human activities, I can take a simple walk on a wild blue line and hear the soothing music that is offered there.

A nation that's divided by hatred and bigotry is way over on one side of the blue line. Paradise, or an unattainable utopia, is way over on the other side. Individually we have the option to walk the line between those places and enjoy it if we choose.

We can be idle there and fearless. In an age of narcissism and the instant "selfie" image, we can even get a portrait of our self as someone charitable and caring. As Robert Louis Stevenson noted in his essay on the idle self, a soul that's balanced with the world is intricate and busy with the wonders of creation.

Before and After Fly-fishing

1

In rethinking the role of wet fly patterns of both the winged and wingless varieties, I've refocused on the time-honored traditions of fishing with an artificial lure. Although I never really abandoned the use of wet flies over my lifetime, I primarily fished like most of my contemporary fly-rod zealots—the folks who love the modern dry fly, nymph and streamer. Over the past few seasons, however, I've been taking a closer look at the old wet fly patterns that have origins extending back to about the fifteenth century.

Wingless wet flies, also known as "soft hackles," appear in one of the first known English books on the subject, *A Treatise of Fishing with an Angle*, ostensibly written in 1496 by the prioress Dame Juliana Berners. With some tying experience under your belt, and with some quality thread and feather, soft hackles can be easy to produce and fun to fish with. There's something appealing about casting with a simple but exquisite pattern like a soft-hackled Orange Fish Hawk or the Partridge and Orange. In my case, learning how to fish these flies effectively helps to broaden the angling horizons again.

The number of wet fly patterns in British and American angling history is immense and overwhelming if you're looking for a place to start. A possible approach would be to read or reread *Trout*, a classic tome by Ray Bergman. I selected a couple of wet flies to study. I chose the Orange Fish Hawk from Bergman's book and found another on the Internet—the obscure Green-Assed McGee. The Green McGee is a pattern once popular in the Pine Creek Valley of Pennsylvania, a home water, and probably nowhere else. I'm a sucker for its link to local history in an area that I frequently haunt.

I also tied a lot of the irresistible Partridge and Orange and the Leisenring Spider, old flies resurrected by the popular book, *The Soft-Hackled Fly*, by Sylvester Nemes, 1975. But for quick immersion in the subject, I focused on the Orange Fish Hawk and the Green-Assed McGee. In a period of deep winter with a case of cabin fever, I was singing the "before and after fly-fishing blues," but was glad to have the tying vise in front of me.

After a bit of a struggle getting the appropriate tying material, I was ready to go. I needed Hungarian partridge feathers for a couple of patterns but readily substituted English grouse. I dove deeper into English and American fly-fishing history, hoping to enrich the present moment. I wanted to keep the study simple.

The Green-Assed McGee apparently had its start in the early twentieth century in the upper Pine Creek Valley. Ostensibly, the name McGee was from an early fly-fisher of north-central Pennsylvania and, as far as I know, he had a normal-colored posterior. It's reported that old-timers liked to fish the fly in tandem with a Muddler Minnow, but the big green fly was also effective when fished alone.

Tied on hook sizes 10 to 14, the McGee has a tail formed out of brown hen fibers. The butt and front end of the body are typically tied from green wool, although red or yellow wool was sometimes used instead. The body's mid-section is a wound strand of peacock herl. Brown fibers can be tied in toward the eye of the hook to represent legs. A dark guinea feather, mottled white, is tied on for a wing. I found that getting decent body proportions with this winged fly was trickier than with the soft-hackle patterns.

The Orange Fish Hawk is a wonderful soft-hackle pattern that is easy to tie. The body of orange floss has a strand of tinsel wound around it, plus a turn or two of soft grizzly hackle. I enjoy tying the old wet fly patterns but, admittedly, my skills remain limited.

As my drive toward angling simplicity muddles onward in a period between two seasons, I will say this: I won't be taking up Tenkara fishing any time soon. Tenkara is an old Japanese approach to fly fishing. Beautiful and very simple, perhaps. But it's suddenly fashionable in the Western world and relies on the purchase of new equipment. Seeing red flags in the air surrounding an already extensive assembly of rods and reels that I enjoy, I resort to my comfort zone and remember Henry Thoreau's dictum, "One life at a time."

2

As a history buff who loves to walk the ageless trail of fly-fishing evolution, I stumbled on a reference to the

Roman writer Aelian who probably recorded the first account of fly-fishing known to literature.

A resident of Rome, Italy, Aelian lived from A.D. 170 to the year 230. Somewhere around 200 A.D., the writer published his *On the Nature of Animals* from which the following excerpts are derived: "I have heard of a Macedonian way of catching fish, and it is this: between Beroea and Thessalonika runs a river called Astraeus, and in it there are fish with speckled skins… These fish feed upon a fly peculiar to the country… In boldness, it is like a fly you might call a midge. It imitates the color of a wasp, and it hums like a bee. The natives call it the *Hippouros*… When the fish observes a fly on the surface, it swims quietly up… It opens its mouth gently and gulps the fly, like a wolf carrying off sheep from the fold… Having done this, it goes below the rippling water…

"The fishermen do not use these flies for bait, for if a man's hand touches them, they lose their natural color, their wings wither, and they become an unfit food for the fish… *They fasten red (crimson red) wool around a hook, and fix onto the wool two feathers which grow under a cock's wattles, and which in color are like wax.*

"Their rod is six feet long, and their line is the same length. Then they throw their snare, and the fish, attracted and maddened by the color, comes straight at it, thinking from the pretty sight to gain a dainty mouthful; when, however, it opens its jaws, it is caught by the hook, and enjoys a bitter repast, a captive."

Although basic fly-fishing may have been practiced in various Eastern lands for many years prior to Aelian's existence, we have something of a first here.

The preceding passages (drawn from Radcliff's *Fishing from the Earliest Times*, 1921, via Dr. Andrew Herd's *flyfishinghistory.com*, and from an adaptation dating back to 1558) suggest the first surviving literary fragment on the venerable craft of fishing with an artificial fly. Grappling with these ancient roots, I worked at the tying vise and finally devised some variations on a first trout fly pattern.

As mentioned on Andrew Herd's web site, the fly pattern described by Aelian is not an imitation of the "midge-like Hippouros fly." Aelian stated that the Hippouros "hovered above the water," and it's possible, as one theory suggests, that he was describing the ascent of a hatched-out mayfly. It's difficult to imagine what the Macedonian Fly really looked like because there's a lot of information that Aelian did not include with his description.

What we know is that the Macedonian anglers tied "red wool around a hook and fixed it with two feathers the color of wax." When we understand that the beeswax of the day was not the color of our bleached contemporary wax, it's probably safe to say that the hackle was brown, or possibly dun. Other tiers have attempted to portray this archetypal fly pattern, and a few of their results can be viewed on-line.

I've tied a few of my own variations on the theme. The exploration isn't the same as having a chance to fly-fish "Macedonia" for river trout in either the second century or the twenty-first, but to think about these roots is a fun trip nonetheless.

If you're interested in fishing the country described by Aelian in his account of the Macedonian Fly, you'll probably need to visit the northern Greek province of Macedonia rather than the Republic of Macedonia, which is north of Greece.

In the time of Aelian, the Greek territory known as Macedonia was frequently at war with the Paeonians who populated what is currently the Republic of Macedonia. Although the Romans artificially expanded the boundaries of Macedonia to include the territory of today's "Republic," Aelian specifically referred to the river Astraeus, the remnants of which can be found in northern Greece. More specifically, strong evidence from recent studies suggests that today's river, the Arapitsas, near Veria, Greece is the river Astraeus that's referred to in the text by Aelian (Grubic and Herd; *The American Fly Fisher*; Fall 2001).

3

I wait for its initial appearance on the rivertops as if it was the season's first robin or woodcock. A hatch of the Little Black Stonefly is assured to make me feel younger than I felt the day before. This fly suggests that spring is here or just around the corner; earth will be green once more, and the air will be stirred by wings.

The Little Black Stonefly is the first of the major aquatic hatches in this area. It ushers in the year's parade of insect hatches over pool and riffle. Other than the winter midges that emerged sporadically on the open water of quiet streams, bug life has been dormant for months. The black stoneflies will emerge from the trout streams soon, and I'll be there to greet them.

On streams like Slate and Cedar Run that tumble into Pennsylvania's Pine Creek Valley, the Little Black Stonefly typically emerges by mid-March (or earlier if the winter has been mild). It precedes the first flush of other significant trout foods like the Early Brown Stonefly and the Blue-winged Olive. Then, by mid-April, come the Blue Quill and the Quill Gordon, followed shortly after by the various caddis and the great mayfly hatches. The stonefly is a gateway hatch, and passing through the gate should remind an angler dulled by winter lethargy that it's great to be alive and reawakened.

The Little Black Stonefly belongs to an order of ancient bugs called *Plecoptera*, the name derived from the Greek "plekein," meaning "braided wings." A stonefly has two pair of wings that rest flatly on its back. The braids, or venation, are obvious on inspection. Of the roughly 550 stonefly species in North America, only a handful should interest the general angler, and the artificial fly patterns can be generic, one pattern covering many similar species.

Stonefly nymphs have a well-developed head, thorax and abdomen, plus an iconic two-part tail. Trout consider them delicacies. Good stonefly populations are an indicator of stream and river health, for these insects do not tolerate pollution.

Stoneflies vary in size and can be tied on hooks ranging from a big #6 down to a small #18, depending on the species that hatch from your local stream. The artificial can be cast successfully throughout the year because the nymphs are always active. The Little Black Stonefly that I'm currently anticipating can be tied on a #14 nymph hook. I like to fish it dead-drift through a deep riffle, on or near the bottom. You might have luck with a dry fly pattern, too, but often when the hatch occurs, the water temperatures remain cold, the flows may still be high and turbid, the trout reluctant to spend great energy for a small reward.

As I meditate on stonefly ecology and the insect's absolute dependence on clean, well-oxygenated water, I digress briefly on a local threat. Advocates for hydrofracking of the gas that's locked below the rivertops give lip service to the health of watersheds, but the industry's performance speaks otherwise. Hydrofracking near the Class A trout streams of rivertop Pennsylvania has been underway for close to a decade as I write. Until recent years, similar operations with attendant infrastructure were a possibility for many New York streams as well. A statement by Sandra Steingraber, a founder of New Yorkers Against Fracking, remains true and pertinent even though the state has, for now, rejected the practice: "Fracking is an accident prone, carcinogen-dependent, climate-destroying enterprise that uses our land as its factory floor and turns our communities into industrial zones."

Stonefly nymphs are abundant in the rivertops that flow down to the north Atlantic, to the Chesapeake and to the Gulf of Mexico. It's hard to be unbiased about fracking practices when I've long resided in a land of headwater streams where stonefly, brook trout, migratory bird, and nature lover dwell in apparent harmony.

"Wherever fracking goes, air is polluted, water is contaminated, roads clog with trucks, property values plummet, and people get sick."

I consider the words by Dr. Steingraber, then listen to the early stoneflies, indicators of excellent water quality. They tell us that another year has opened on a healthy note, that evolution still exists as nature intended. Stoneflies also tell us that angling is a varied subject and deals with more than simply catching fish. They say that it's good to belong to a special place, a natural environment of our choosing.

4

I felt like committing some random acts of small stream fishing. I felt like driving toward the headwaters while rocking out to some Richard Thompson music caught on tape. I listened to three consecutive songs from the "History of Richard Thompson, Vol. 2," from the great British guitarist who once headed the rock band Fairport Convention in its early days, and wondered again if there were any three consecutive songs in the archives of recorded modern music more powerful emotionally than "Borrowed Time," "From Galway to Graceland," and "Tear-Stained Letter." If so, I didn't know of them.

The first song, recorded in 1979, is simply insightful rock-and-roll. The second, from 1990, is a spot-on ballad and a portrait of total schizophrenia. The third song (1991) highlights the folk themes that Thompson has mastered over the years, plus his soaring instrumental prowess. As one of rock's finest songwriters and guitarists, Thompson reminds me why music is so important to my love for writing and fly-fishing. It brings together the continuity of time, of years gone by, along with the present moment and the possibilities of the future. It provides me with a sense of freedom and the beauty of nature amplified.

Out of the dazzling skies of April and my own sense of wayward determinism, I decided to fish the middle branch of my home river where the old meadows studded with white pine trees lend a portrait of scenic value. Sadly enough, I didn't catch any trout there but, walking back to my parked vehicle, I stepped across a tiny brook as I've done in years past, with one exception—I paused.

The rivulet feeding the Middle Branch, like numerous others, was green with cress and flowing over sand and gravel. It looked like a home for native trout… What if….

I started following this "step across stream" toward the highway. With an underhand swing, I dropped a weighted fly into the narrow channel. The brook was too small for any other type of casting. I didn't recall ever seeing a thin blue line on the topographic map suggesting a feeder stream at this location. This was certainly one of the tiniest brooks I have ever bothered to drop a line on.

The channel averaged only two feet wide, its depth about a foot. A fish bumped the fly but didn't hold. A bit farther on, a second fish struck from the cress but disappeared. I was getting close to the highway culvert and a probable source from a spring beyond. Passing cars probably thought me daft as a rock to be casting in a field "without any water nearby."

This fool for trout finally captured and released a pair of pretty natives from the wet grass near the culvert. Ah, who would have known… or even cared? But it was spring, and there was water music in the air.

While driving home, I listened to parts of Handel's jolly "Water Music Suite" on National Public Radio. England's King George had heard an early version of this music while floating the Thames on an orchestral barge. I was hearing something different here, where evening frogs chorused from a marsh that I was passing through. Birds were singing, also, and through it all came the memory of trout.

5

After a brief illness, I drank (poetically speaking) from the clear streams and rivers of my life, and they made me well. The blossom of a trout lily was there.

Trout Unlimited and representatives from the Youth of America gathered on the banks of a tributary to the upper Genesee. We planted more than a thousand trees, small willows, pine, sycamore, and oak. A trout lily was there.

I fly-fished on the upper Allegheny, catching and releasing wild brooks and browns and stocked rainbow trout. The water temperature climbed to 52 degrees; the Quill Gordons and the first Hendrickson mayflies appeared. A trout lily was there.

I swung over to the Pine Creek watershed, the third river system in my Three River Rise… I walked the old railroad grade. A camper told me of a great black bear that had ambled along the creek the previous moon-lit night and passed right by his outdoor fire. And by morning, a trout lily was there.

On a feeder stream, I caught brookie after brookie on a Hare's Ear nymph, getting my fix of the wild at Splash Dam Hollow. Ah, the blossoms with their leaves patterned like the back of a fish! A trout lily was there.

I drove down to the canyon, rigging up three wet flies like the old-timers used to do. I'm the old-timer now, and it works, sort of—Muddler Minnow for the point fly, a Hare's Ear and a Green-Assed McGee for droppers... With a long rod, it seemed more like casting for steelhead than for brooks—across and down through the deep wide riffle... and you bet, a trout lily was there.

I remembered a time in the early 1980s when I rode a rickety bus through the boulder-studded mountains of Epirus in northern Greece. I wasn't fishing at the time, but thought, wouldn't it be interesting to find wild trout in these fabulous mountain brooks where seemingly no one knows or cares about fly-fishing?

Recently I learned that fly-fishing for trout is becoming recognized for its recreational and economic potential in iconic northern Greece, particularly in the region near the fabled Astraeus, the river that inspired a first literary mention of angling with an artificial fly (by Aelian, ca. 200 A.D.).

I've read that as late as the year 2013 most of the fishermen in northern Greece were casting with hardware or (yes) still using such deplorable devices as TNT to gather a meal of trout. Ostensibly in the year 2013, there were about 30 fly-fishermen in all of Greece. Luckily for us, however, that number is growing rapidly, especially among the younger generation.

At my age, I doubt I'll ever have the chance to revisit the bountiful freestone or limestone-kissed waters of rocky Epirus or Macedonia that gave birth to the craft of fly-fishing for trout, and that's okay with me. I'll be gone, but content to know that a trout lily, or

a Grecian bloom equivalent in beauty and significance,
blossoms on a bank nearby.

Upper Kettle, Sunday

1

The weather could not have been finer—a bluebird sky, a slight breeze comfortable when I wore a t-shirt and a fishing vest. This was the weekend I'd been looking for—with songbirds in the sycamores and willows, with tiger swallowtails wafting over the sparkling riffles, and with Sulphurs and Green Drakes hatching over hungry trout.

The Kettle Creek water registered a cool 52 degrees on Saturday morning. A dry fly was ignored at first, but at the B&B Pool everything changed. I switched to an emerger pattern and quickly netted a strange-looking rainbow with heft. Oddly enough, the trout had some characteristics of a brown, or so I thought, and thus I dubbed it my *"brainbow"* trout.

I was ready to engage the many wild brook trout in this stretch of water, but I waded into a knot of bait and spin-cast fellows so made a detour around them. Watching a high-flying eagle soaring toward a western hollow, I followed it, in a sense, and entered the big woods.

The small tributary in the hollow is a Class A wild trout stream. Hardly anyone knows of its existence, to my reckoning. I've yet to see any sign of human presence there. The forest understory is relatively clear, and it's fun to cast a fly rod over the little stream. Unfortunately, on this occasion, the 8-foot rod I carried was considerably longer than preferred.

Most of the miniature pools contained a small brook trout or two. By the time I reached the mountain's shoulder, I lost track of how many speckled fish had risen to the dry fly, an irresistible Stimulator that floated perfectly.

Upon returning to Kettle Creek and finding a sporadic hatch of Green Drake mayflies, I tied on a large imitation called the Grey Fox Variant and continued to catch and release wild brookies. The native fish seem to be thriving here despite the stocking of hatchery trout and a steady pressure of bait and spinning anglers not averse to bringing home a limit now and then.

The forest has returned to the mountainsides along much of the creek. More and more anglers are returning most of what they catch. Downstream, habitat improvement projects have been completed by sportsmen and conservation groups. The result is a 40-mile stream that's starting to resemble the way it looked and fished in its glory days of the nineteenth century.

The entirety of the Kettle Creek watershed in northern Pennsylvania had been known as one of the finest brook trout regions in the country prior to its transformation by the lumbering and mining operations around the turn of the twentieth century. Then, its wild fish grew to sizes well above a foot in length, with occasional specimens reaching 18 inches. Although a 12-inch native trout might be considered an outstanding wild fish today, I had moments on the Kettle when I thought I saw the glory of the stream that was.

Sunday on the Kettle was a mirror image of the day before. I was upstream of the previous site and there I got my fix for wildness by ascending another small feeder stream in a roadless area of scenic beauty. I carried a 7-foot rod and, once again, had many brook trout rise from the pools and undercuts and riffled waters. This stream was managed by the state as Brook Trout Enhancement water until the regulations were recently changed to Catch-and-Release, All Tackle. All other tributaries, including the Kettle itself, are managed as such from here on upstream to the sources of the watershed. There's no closed season for wild brooks and browns, but the fishing is strictly catch-and-release.

The farther I walked into this wild area, the better the dry fly fishing became. Back on Kettle in the early evening, I saw no other anglers. A few bugs were hatching, and once again my choice of imitation for the fine end of the leader was the Grey Fox Variant, as tied by the late Art Flick.

I had one recurrent thought that acted as a weekend theme—given the excellent weather, plus the hatching flies, the hungry trout, and the scenic setting—there was no place anywhere that I would rather be fishing. There was no place anywhere, at least for today.

2

One year I arrived at Kettle for my tradition of casting through the long Memorial Day weekend and found that the stream was in fine shape following a spate of mid-week rains. It was only 12 o'clock noon but already the mayflies were fluttering off the water.

At first I saw the "greys"—the Grey Fox, a light-colored version of the March Brown mayfly, and then came the "greens"—the famous Green Drake, followed by the smaller yellowish mayfly commonly known as a Sulphur. This trifecta brought the songbirds out of the willow trees, as well. Catbirds and yellow warblers swooped down over the tumbling stream to scarf up their lunches, an evanescent fluttering on the breeze.

Experimentation told me that the brooks, browns and rainbows were feeding on the surface for the most part and preferring the dry fly over the wets and nymphs, at least for now. For eastern waters, this was dry fly fishing at its annual peak in late May, and I was knee-deep in one of my favorite streams.

Before the hatch activity shut down in late afternoon, I had caught and freed several dozen trout, mostly brooks, both stocked and wild. Aside from the natives, I had also reeled in several hefty browns and a brace of 15-inch rainbows. The larger specimens were fun to catch, but of special interest to me were the healthy brook trout. They were wild fish larger than average size for Pennsylvania.

Along one of the braided sections of the creek where several feeder streams entered close by, I watched a bald eagle perching in a sycamore tree. I was hoping to approach close enough for a photo, but I was catching fish while trying to keep my arm and leg movements at a minimum. I didn't want to frighten the eagle but the fun of it all was like burning a candle at both ends.

When the largest of my brook trout came to the net, I saw that it was close to a foot in length, and rich with color—its orange, green and red hues like that of a spawning male in autumn. While struggling for a quick photo of the trout, I alerted the mature bald eagle, which then took wing. The trout was released, and I swung the camera over my head as the eagle passed by. All I got was an image of a regal white tail and the blur of a wing beneath the vast blue sky. The result reminded me of the bigger picture—while fishing, or living out our daily lives, all we usually catch is a fragment of reality. If we're lucky or make good use of what we've learned in the past, we're served a little piece of the moment's pie, and that's it. If we can the taste the sweetness therein, and imagine the rest, I guess that's good enough.

3

May 31: The morning trout were rising, and again I struggled to decipher the hatch that raised them. Finally, I figured it out. Midges again, dammit. But thankfully the overcast conditions soon delivered a larger fly that came through like a hero. Quickly replacing a #22 Midge with a "normal" imitation, a size 18 Blue-winged Olive, I began to have some fun. Oh, I still got plenty of refusals, but at least I tangled with a few good brown trout and even a wild brookie at the beautiful bend pool. I never saw much of the anticipated Sulphurs or Green Drakes today, but the Olives saved me from frustration.

June 6: The sun shone brightly on the upper Kettle. Insects, for the most part, were slumbering. I saw a couple of Drakes, and that was it, but the trout rose for an imitation nonetheless. It was fun to hook up with the hatchery browns and rainbows, and a lot of small brook trout as well.

I didn't need to play the hatch game today, oddly enough. Matching the hatch is what serious fly-flingers do from time to time, especially now in rivertop country when any number of caddis, stonefly or mayfly hatches can occur daily. Sometimes trout become very selective in their feeding habits, so on these occasions the angler would do well to match the given hatch in color, size and profile. As much as I enjoy matching the artificial to a natural insect, today I enjoyed not having to deal with fussy eating habits even more.

June 7: What a difference a day makes. This morning the bugs (the non-biters) were everywhere—emergers, duns and spinners—and the trout were feeding mainly on the Blue-winged Olive that the Kettle is renowned for on June mornings.

The weather couldn't have been more comfortable or bright. Hooked rainbows leapt above the water. In the Ledge Pool, well upstream from the special regulations area where most of the fly-fishers congregated, healthy browns fed quietly at the surface.

There was sweetness in the air, perhaps from the resins of hemlock or pine, or from the blooms of various wildflowers, reminding me of Rocky Mountain summer streams. A male scarlet tanager sang its hoarse robin-like song from high in a creek-side maple.

I quit fishing after trout 18. I'd seen a mix of larger-than-average stockers and wild brook trout. It was the kind of day I dreamed about in February. It was match-the-hatch, catch-and-release fishing that the non-angler or the bait-fisher might construe as rarified or even elitist, but wait… there's more…

I sympathized with several worm-casters I spoke with. They had seen the passing of their hour in the sun. For the most part, trout ignored their offerings now that flies had become top items for the daytime feed. These were guys who claimed to release a big portion of their trout but who admitted that a swallowed hook killed fish. I reminded them that fly-fishing would extend their season if they liked it, but I came off sounding rather lame and unconvincing.

I don't like to be so involved with trout behavior that I seem as fussy as selective browns. I don't want to miss out on the other stuff that happens in the neighborhood, like the mourning warbler chatting in the understory; the monarch butterfly sipping at water's edge, or the black bear keeping an eye on the angler's desperate trout.

To help maintain my balance today I tried to keep my eyes and ears open, as well as to sing a little to myself—a gutsy rock 'n' roll lyric or some improvised jazz. To function as my own audience is sort of schizophrenic, I suppose, but at least I keep myself from getting lonely.

4

One Sunday morning in late September I resettled on Kettle Creek's headwaters after an absence of several years. The scenery and the fishing were outstanding.

I remembered a spring day on the headwaters when I caught and released 64 trout along a mile of stream in this location, the most I've ever bothered counting in a single day. I've gone back to this stretch of water numerous times (a special regulations stream where all brook trout must be returned unharmed) and not done nearly as well. No doubt there were also times when the stream sent me home with my head bowed and with tail between my legs, but on this most recent occasion I did well. My catch rate seemed as high as on that magical day in spring but I fished only half as long.

I'd been following the massive caddis hatches over the previous week or so, and found that a small dry Adams was the only fly I needed on the upper Kettle. Other good floating patterns might have worked just as well. The sun shone in a flawless sky and on the brightening forest. The spawning season for native trout put color on the smooth skin, especially on the larger males.

It was Sunday, and contentment gripped the soul. The mountain valley and its stream were like a church for me. I waded underneath a blue-sky steeple, by the walls of colored foliage, while communing in my own way with the fishes. Solitude and comfort made it easy.

Someday I'll be dead and gone, but not to a place any better or worse. My confidence is based on natural observation. The word "God" is not a factor for me, but *Energy* is. I think of William Blake's declaration, "Energy is Eternal Delight." When I'm gone, the mountain stream will flow just as purely, if not more so, and that's good enough for me.

I believe it was Alfred W. Miller (a.k.a. Sparse Grey Hackle) who wrote, in effect, that the time to fish and to love is now, because this is all we've got. "You can't go fishing in Greenlawn Cemetery." Smart guy, that Mr. Miller, the author of *Fishless Days, Angling Nights*.

The upper Kettle and its feeders have about 30 miles of specially regulated catch-and-release fishing. Angling is an all-year opportunity here, but every brown and brook trout must be safely returned to the stream. Prior to forest and mining devastation in the early twentieth century, Kettle was among the finest brook trout waters anywhere. Today, with special fishing regulations and some major restoration projects along its wooded banks, the creek is improving and doing well, all things considered. The strain of native trout isn't the same as it was originally, and the fish don't get as large, but the population in the headwaters is substantial.

I saw what appeared to be another typical brook trout in front of me at the tail of a pool. I made a short cast, placing the dry fly several feet upstream of the fish. The trout rose and took the presentation. A flash of color and the feel of weight told me that it wasn't like the others.

I thrust the net beneath and lifted. An exemplary male, with brightness and heft. I took a photograph and touched the smooth, cool skin. The trout gave me its share of beauty in the world, and I gave it a shot of needed energy in return. I watched it swim away to the protection of an overhang. From there, the trout would paint my afternoon.

The King, the Spider, and the Rise

Sometimes our experiences far afield come back and influence the way we fish, and live, at home. Since few of us are truly native to our adopted lands, it's good to be influenced positively by the great traditions of our sport or the passions rooted in a distant locale. In the case of angling on the waters of home, I'm reminded of several prominent fly patterns that have entered my life from distant locales to help guide the way I fish.

1

The last thing I expected to see along a headwaters stream in the Pecos Wilderness was another angler. There were mobs of them on the main flow down below Terrero where the hatchery fish are dumped, but up here in cutthroat country, forget it. I was releasing a Rio Grande cutt to its rightful habitat when I glanced toward the bank. My physical response was like being kicked in the ass by a grizzly bear…

"Oh, hey, h-how's it going?" I stammered at the fisherman. We exchanged brief greetings and updates on our fishing luck. Oddly enough, we both claimed to have caught and released about 10 of the beautifully colored trout that once ranged over much of the Sangre de Christo Mountains in Colorado and New Mexico.

"What you taking them on?" asked the young Latino fly-fisher who lived west of Santa Fe.

"Royal Wulff," I said. "A good floater on this wicked little stream."

"I like using a Rio Grande King," he said. "A good floater, like the Wulff, plus it's easy to follow and easy to tie. Here, take one." I had heard of the pattern, glanced at pictures of the fly, but had never actually fished or even seen one back East. I gave the pattern an inspection.

Hook: #14 dry fly. Tail: fibers of golden pheasant tail. Body: black chenille. Wing: tuft of white calf or deer hair. Hackle: dark brown. Origin: possibly Denver, Colorado, early 1900s. Portrayed in Ray Bergman's book *Trout*, 1938.

A fluffy non-descript pattern, resembling nothing in a trout's diet that we can speak of with assurance. As a wet fly or a dry, the King works well both far and wide. I've learned that it's effective on the Test in England and on the Pecos in New Mexico. I'll have some great success with it on Eastern streams like Dyke Creek and Cedar Run when trout are rising for black ants on the surface.

"Which way you fishing?" inquired the well-informed angler of the Rio Grande watershed.

"Heading upstream, but please, jump in anywhere you want," I said.

"I'll walk up a way and give you plenty of room," he added.

"Thank you for the fly, and good luck!"

So, I tied the angler's Rio Grande King to my tippet and resumed my slow trek along this most challenging of rivertop streams. Whether I gave the fly an underhand swing, a bow shot, or a forward cast, it raised fish after fish. Before I lost it to an unforgiving branch, the fly took several regal-looking Rio Grandes, a rare subspecies of cutthroat trout, a fish to be studied quickly and released.

As a footnote to this anecdote about the fly that I've described, I want to say that soon after my experience on the upper Pecos River, I wrote about the "King" on my fly-fishing blog called *Rivertop Rambles.* Miraculously enough, I got a couple of interesting responses to my post, the first of which came from a young man named Antonio, who wrote:

Mr. Franklin,

I googled Pecos Wilderness looking to see if there was public access to a small creek, and this blog was the second on the Google list. I just by chance read it because it had to do with [No Name Creek] and while reading the entry realized that it reflected our encounter up there. I will keep in touch, and have added this blog to my faves to see how your adventures play out. Take care...

And thus began a valued correspondence between myself and Antonio, who introduced me to the Rio Grande King. I'd like to include here a part of my initial response to Antonio via my blog:

...Sometimes I think that new technology is collapsing the world all too quickly, but in this case I am thankful for the fast connections. The road trip to New Mexico convinced me that the physical world remains a very big place... If you ever feel like sending

a report of your fishing experiences out there, I'd surely welcome a read...

A second response to my post about the King came from Ed C., in Oregon:

Enjoyed your post about the Rio Grande King... My late father showed me this fly in Eastern Oregon about 40 years ago. It was literally the only fly we used on the Chewaucan River in Lake County Oregon. From spring through early fall, whether in early morning or in late afternoon, it always caught fish. Thank you for the details. I've been unable to find the fly here in southwest Oregon...

With a little help from new friends, the King entered my life at the Triple Divide.

2

The wet fly patterns known as "North Country Spiders" came to prominence in England around 1885 with the publication of *Yorkshire Trout Flies* written by T.E. Pritt. But some of the spider patterns had been around for a long while prior to the nineteenth century. Say, three or four centuries before the publication of Pritt's fishing book. The spiders rank among the first recorded patterns in British fly-fishing history and remain popular in many parts of the modern fly-fishing realm.

North Country Spiders are elegant, simple, and effective in their use for trout. Ironically, they have very little to do with arachnids. Their generic name stems from the hackles that are wound around the upper hook. The hackles are soft feathers taken from a grouse or a partridge and wrapped once or twice around a thin, short body. The hackle may resemble the legs of spiders, but even more so, they represent the legs and wings of insects hatching just below the surface of water. On one hand, the flies may imitate emerging bugs while, on the other hand, they could be mistaken for dead or dying adults.

The success of these patterns is largely due to the movement of hackle in each push or pull of water current. Soft hackle responds like the movement of natural body parts. The imitations are sparsely dressed. They are generally fished near the surface where the "legs" lie tightly at the body's side, moving forward when the drift begins to slow.

I'm not sure what inspired me to suddenly tie some spiders but I think it had to do with the Vernal Equinox. It was the first day of spring but the weather looked anything other than spring-like. A driving snowfall kept me near the wood stove in the afternoon. Minutes passed, and the snow gave way to a burst of golden sunlight and a dearth of wind. I went outside and walked in very different weather, but the sun didn't last long. Wind and snow returned, so I went back to the tying vise.

I wanted to produce something that was spare and simple, something to give me hope on the trout streams in the weeks to come. I needed something made by my own average hands, something with a link to a season that was all too slow in getting here.

I said, "North Country Spiders" and I thought of the various northern districts of England giving slow birth to the fly patterns that survive today. There was music to be heard while wrapping silken threads around a wet fly hook. There was music in the search for an adequate hackle to wind in front of a dubbed thorax.

I thought of Brian Eno's song called "Spider and I." It's an easy song to hum to, and the lyrics are deceptively simple... *Spider and I/ sit watching the sky/ on a world without sound,/ Knitting a web / to catch one tiny fly/ for a world without sound./ We sleep in the morning./ We dream of a ship/ that sails away/ a thousand miles away....*

The song is from the album "Before and After Science," which I've enjoyed since hearing it on vinyl back in the late 1970s. If you check out the comments for the song at You Tube music, you might discover blurbs such as, "The best song about a spider ever written," or "One of the most beautiful songs in the history of rock." It's hard for me to argue such sentiments. Written in 1977, amidst the welter of a very different punk rock universe, "Spider and I," like other work from the 1970s Eno canon, proves that beautiful, expansive music can last for many years and motivate a clumsy hand at the fly-tying vise.

When I held a bunch of newly tied spiders in my hand, I saw that they looked a bit ratty and overdressed, but the hint of elegance was there nonetheless. They pointed to a fine spring day in April or in June, and I knew them to be small but important links to the early chapters in the history of fly-fishing, like a ship that sails away, not quite "a thousand miles away."

3

We can state, with reasonable accuracy, that what a trout sees in the water is a far cry from what we ourselves might see under similar circumstances. So, what value does incorporating a new trout fly pattern into our fishing habits have on productivity? Does the casting of a new fly, say, a Rio Grande King or a type of Spider, make any real difference in the way we fish? Perhaps it does, or maybe it doesn't. Instead of concerning ourselves with specific views, as in what a trout may see while looking toward the surface of a stream, we might do better by considering generalities.

For a week or so I'd been anxiously awaiting a good Hendrickson hatch, the mayfly whose appearance on Eastern streams and rivers tends to produce good dry fly action on the surface of the water. Although the air and water temperatures of early spring had been warm enough for both trout and angler, the afternoon skies had been unusually bright, and the mayfly's appearance had been minimal. Undaunted by the lack of dry fly action, I sought the trout at a deeper level of the water column.

I'm not a dry fly purist and I'm not afraid to run a streamer through the deeper waters of a trout lair. Since I don't presume to know exactly what a trout can see (half the time I can't be sure exactly what it is that *I am seeing*, even when stone sober), I can only speculate on the nature of another creature's vision.

When the sky is blue and the water filled with sunshine, it's a fair bet that a trout, not blessed with an eye-lid that can block the light, would rather not search for insects hatching directly overhead. In that case, it probably wouldn't matter if we made a perfect delivery of an Elk Hair Caddis, a Rio Grande King, or an Orange Fish Hawk—if the fly was intended to float on or near the surface, a trout would not be interested. That said, a large trout, even if it tends to feed mostly after dark, isn't always napping during the daylight hours.

A juicy-looking bucktail or a streamer drifted enticingly through the depths might spur a strike if the fish doesn't need to leave its lair of safety for long. In other words, if the angler can present a lure convincingly within the safety zone, there's a good chance for a strike when other signs for decent angling are about as scarce as honest politicians.

When conditions don't favor a specific strategy (such as one we had hoped to employ) we shouldn't hesitate to try another approach that's recommended by good sense and judgement. When I approached a series of tressel-bridge pools at the mid-section of Dyke Creek in the Genesee River watershed and found very little hatch activity under the bright May Day sky, something told me to switch leaders and to tie on a weighted Muddler Minnow.

Within minutes of allowing the streamer to drift and twitch along an unfathomed pool, I was on to my heaviest brown trout of the season so far. The fish was a battler, a tough one to net, despite its modest length.

It would soon be time for the March Browns to appear, a mayfly that is possibly even more significant to the angler than the Hendrickson. I'd be looking for the large brown fly within a week or so, although the long-range weather forecast called for a continuation of warm days and clear blue skies, conditions that sounded favorable to all but the serious fisherman. If I didn't see the hatches that I hoped to find, no matter. The trout would be seeing something other than what I could perceive, anyway.

For example, the trout might key in on nymphs loosened from the bedrock; they might focus on caddis rising toward the surface; they might partake in any number of hatching possibilities. At a time like this, it might be good for an angler to experiment with that new fly in the arsenal, to try the Rio Grande King or that old world spider known as the Partridge and Orange. There's only that mystery hidden in the watery depths to tell us if the fly will work or not.

A Spring Creek Journal

December 5: I hadn't fished Spring Creek in upstate New York for several years, so I jumped at an opportunity to revisit the limestone water on a warm day in early December. Unlike central and southern Pennsylvania where spring creeks (aka limestone creeks) are renowned throughout the angling world, upstate New York has very few of these special waters.

I'll define a spring creek here as one with a limestone base that serves cold water through the year at a relatively uniform temperature, with a food supply that tends to grow large healthy trout suspicious of any morsel with a hook. The spring creek nearest to my home flows northward into Oatka Creek and Lake Ontario, and is probably the finest of its kind in the upstate region.

This type of trout stream isn't as common as you might think. It's been estimated that, of all the flowing trout water available in the world, less than one-thousandths of that volume is in the form of a limestone run.

There's a state hatchery located on the creek, and nearly all the fish above and below the hatchery are wild (excepting the occasional escapee) brook and brown trout. From an angler's point of view, these trout seem highly "educated," unable to be pigeon-holed as pushover specimens. They can be extremely selective in what they rise to or nibble at among the gardens of lush green watercress. To fly-fish successfully at this location, or at any similar limestone water on the planet, it would help the angler to have a minimum of the following characteristics, to one degree or another: an ability to observe feeding trout, to hold patience in reserve, to have a willingness to experiment with flies and leader tippets, and to know a love for the peace and quiet of a special locale.

Most of Spring Creek flows through private property of an upstate village, but there are a few points of public access, limited, for sure, and very popular, so it's especially important for an interested angler to understand the special regulations in effect for the stream and to hone his points of ethical consideration. Fishermen can work the hatchery grounds at Caledonia during business hours, or cast below the hatchery on a stretch of water called the "900s," a local term for the popular 900-plus yards of public access beginning at a point near the railroad bridge.

There isn't much room to fish here, so etiquette is paramount. Most of the anglers I've encountered on the creek are conscientious people willing to sacrifice mobility so that the next guy doesn't feel too crowded. But maybe I shouldn't sound too optimistic or be tempting the cruel hands of fate. I fish this jewel of a trout stream only during the winter months when angling pressure is light and there's usually plenty of room to cast. I can't imagine what it's like in May or June when the insect hatch is more diverse than the winter midge supply, and when I'm able to be off rambling on a mountain stream somewhere.

Right from the start this day, I saw fish rising to midges and forming rings on the surface of a pool, or making boils of water just beneath the film. Occasionally a trout would throttle up and out, as if chasing an emergent caddis. I began my work by laying out a 10-foot leader tapered to a thin 7X point, but I couldn't get a fish to take anywhere near the surface. I attempted to connect by casting every form of midge in the arsenal, from big #18s to miniscule #24s, from dry fly to pupa, and nothing worked. The hours flowed by with little more than a tug on my smallest Gnat, but then I changed my strategy and prepared a Grey Scud, #14 hook.

My lesson learned: If you finesse things too much, you can come up empty-handed. "The Tao that can be named is not the eternal Tao," to quote from a great philosophical treatise composed in the sixth-century B.C. The Spring Creek way is not the way it was or will be. Today the trout went for the "big hook" (Scud) drifting along the bottom; tomorrow they could be sipping #28s in the surface film.

The last fish of the day was the one I hoped would pose for a photograph. It was the fish that got released too early. I'd felt the take of a heavy brown and then my moves with the trout became a rodeo scene. I'd set the hook with a sharp lift of an arm. I reeled in the line and pivoted as the brown raced at me and into the rocks behind my back. Holding up the rod, I fumbled for the net with my left hand and then made a feeble attempt to pull the camera from a zipped-up pocket in my vest. I began to lift the trout from its shelter in the rocks.

Wrong move! You should *never* lift a heavy trout by the leader, not if you plan on having a good look at your catch. It's like wrestling a steer by the horns, I guess, then letting go before the beef is tired. So, the rock's edge split my leader and that was it, but not before I had a nice look at a gorgeous buttery-toned brown trout.

There are big fish living in the beds of grass, but usually what you see are the small ones, lots of them, living wild and colorful existences among the weaving grasses and conflicting currents. I try to be gentle with these fish and release them for another day among their kind, and lasso up some memories.

January 15: My fishing partner had a nice wild brown trout on the line, so I waded into the Oatka at a point where Spring Creek feeds it with its limestone magic, and there I floundered into the drink. That is, I went under while in the clutches of a rising creek, just downstream of the fishing action. Regaining my feet on solid ground, I was lucky that the air on this January day was relatively warm, about the same temperature as the water when I took the photograph of Tim's 17-inch trout. But let me say, I'm glad that my immersion in the stream was the less-than-grand finale for the day and hadn't happened earlier. As it was, I drove home with the heat cranked high, and with my clothes as wet as a fish.

The morning had begun with a sense of quiet majesty. An adult bald eagle flew in front of me as I left the Town of Greenwood. On arrival at the creek, Tim and I viewed the movements of trout beneath the railroad bridge at Spring Creek. I began to fish at the upper end of the public water and Tim moved downstream past several other fly-fishers to the lowest beat of the "900s." The sun appeared dimly and began to melt the banks of snow.

I tied a #14 Hare's Ear to the 5X point of a 9-foot leader. To that, I added a #16 Scud on a foot of 6X tippet and then I topped off this crazy rig with a #22 Midge Emerger fastened to a length of 7X. Each of the flies had a bead head, and my 8-foot cane rod delivered them without a snarl. Eventually a half dozen trout, wild brooks and browns, came out for the quick release. Each of them had taken the smallest fly, the brown midge that Tim had given me before we left the car.

When we decided to have a look at the Oatka down below the point where Spring Creek enters that fishery, the water was rising fast from the snowmelt. It was nearly bank-full and the color of coffee ice cream. We were there, so hastened to give it a shot, replacing 7X or 8X leader tippets with steelhead gut and a streamer or two. It felt treacherous stepping three feet into the creek and not knowing where the next step might be leading, so we turned around and headed back up to the junction pool where Spring Creek makes its entrance.

I saw a fish in the seam where clear water mixed into brown Oatka. Stepping to a depth that reached my knees, I let the streamer drift and come to a halt. At first the weight felt like a rolling log. I pulled a massive sucker from the water and, with a laugh, raised it for a photo on Tim's camera. Sucker and I returned to the intriguing seam of water. That's when Tim shouted. It was his turn. No doubt this one would be worth a picture, so I pivoted in the flow and lost my balance with a tumble to my knees and then to my neck.

As I mentioned earlier, the water was winter cold, and only my nose and hat stayed relatively dry.

February 21: When I arrived at the tiny, garage-sized parking lot provided by the state, I found it filled with four other vehicles. Squeezing in on the ice, I suited up and began the short walk to that rare upstate commodity—a good trout stream free of ice in winter, thanks to the relatively constant water temperature throughout the year.

Fishing space was limited, but the good news here is that no matter where you stand, you'll see fish. To catch them is another issue altogether. The wild brown trout here have seen it all, and they're often smart enough to deflate the egos of the most experienced angler.

Throughout the morning, I tempted the fish with all the usual suspects—midges, streamers, scuds, emergers, and soft-hackles—without luck. I had to listen to anglers talking about their jobs, their marriages, and their fishing successes—all of which are fine, of course, until you can't turn them off with the simple act of catching fish.

Then came the turn-around. I managed to make myself warm and comfortable and more confident in my abilities. There was one fly in the boxes that I hadn't yet tried. I tied it to the 6X tippet point and fastened a split-shot well above the fly. I focused on a good-looking fish, and it took. At last.

In the next 90 minutes, I caught and let go another half a dozen browns, most of them well above a foot in length. Wild and beautifully toned, the trout seemed well-conditioned by the excellent nutrients synonymous with limestone flows.

Driving home, I encountered strong winds and a mix of rain and snow. With a month of northern winter still ahead of me, it was good to have swallowed a shot of spring creek tonic for whatever comes my way.

March 10: Along with NPR's early morning broadcast of an ancient hymn, I heard the first sweet phrases of a migrant robin near the yard, so I stepped to the porch in my bare feet for a clearer sound of both music sources, and thought, *at last…* a fine day to fish Spring Creek again, even if later in the day the air would be chilly and the sky deeply overcast.

I quickly landed and released a wild brown measuring a full-net 15 inches. Hours later, just before departing from this limestone creek, I hooked into a larger brown that took me downstream and sliced the tippet from a 10-foot leader. In between these fishes, I enjoyed the company of eight other trout that took the bottom-drifting, orange or pink-hued flies.

I'm not complaining, but I've got to mention the midday hatch of midges. These tiny, non-biting *Chironomidae* are two-winged creatures of slow, weedy streams that can hatch at any time of year. Good news! A hatch of winter flies resembling small mosquitoes means… dry-fly fishing, right? Well, sort of. Spring Creek has a way of talking to an angler who gets excited about such prospects. The stream says, "Hold on to your tippet, friend. If anyone commands the center of gravity here, it's me, not the visitor."

Trout were rising at the time, and one of them readily seized a #20 Griffith's Gnat, a small fly big enough to be mistaken for a couple of black gnats fused together, either by accident or buggy lust. The trout leapt from the water a couple of times and was gone. And that was as close as I came to capturing my first trout of the season on a dry fly.

All subsequent surface presentations were refused. A Black Midge #20 was too small and dark for me to follow on the water, and too damn large to be considered seriously by the midge-eaters. After my frozen fingers managed to rebuild a leader tippet, I found live midges crawling underneath the gloves I'd laid down on a log.

Comparing the live midges to my artificial fly, I found the live bugs to be roughly half the size of what I'd been casting and was willing to tie on the leader point. Seeing the problem of my cold, unwilling fingers, and a breeze that maddened both line and leader, I knew that dry flies weren't about to connect with these rising fish.

That's not to say that I didn't become obsessed with trying. A size #24 Gnat was the right size but the wrong color, apparently. I could see the darned thing on the surface but felt that, as with emergent patterns, I would almost need to place it into the trout's mouth before getting a fish to strike. It wasn't a lot of fun, and it slowly drove me bonkers.

Fish kept rising, and I finally said to hell with it, I'm going back to a Scud. Pink and orange were suitable colors for the artificial fly. I had good action while casting a 3-weight line with a rod long enough to manage the tricky current seams.

The birds weren't singing anymore but occasionally the ducks would fly overhead and a muskrat would emerge from its den. When a great blue heron pulled up on the bank nearby and asked in its peculiar avian way if it would be alright to fish, I grumbled my assent. After all, the heron and other creatures belonged to this place long before I had come around.

Aside from the midges, I had no reason to complain.

March 16: Saturday looked like the best of the weekend for a final shot at fishing Spring Creek for this season. I'd had good luck here on several winter outings this year, so I approached the water calmly, ready to accept whatever fate was dealing. Although the upstate weather forecast had predicted a high around 40 degrees, I would find that intermittent rain and snow squalls put a damper on the pleasure principle.

I'd been taken to task the week before by the midges on this stream. I now intended to ignore them, mostly, and try to figure an alternative strategy for success. A small hatch of midges did occur at midday, and a few trout sipped at the adults on or near the surface, but the action was minimal enough to stay calm and collected. I was lucky for that. My gloves were in the car (again) and my hands were numbed to the point where I would have failed at tying on a 7X leader tippet for the midge-sized artificials.

So, I worked at casting tandem flies on a 10-foot leader. With a split-shot pulling down an Egg or a Scud for a point fly, I also drifted an accompanying Pheasant-tail Nymph or a Midge Pupa. Eventually I caught and released nine trout, while losing about the same number.

For whatever reason, each trout was taken on the point fly. They were all wild browns, mostly in the 11 to 15-inch range. As always, one of the fish that got away was the most memorable of the outing.

As another angler pointed out, the ones that get away are usually big, or special. My favorite of the day was estimated to be around 18 inches long, which means that, really, it was close to 16 inches, but felt like a 20 as it rolled around the surface water and then absconded with the fly.

As the scientific closure of winter held me in thrall, the wild browns fed as if spring was all that mattered now. The Equinox was closing in, at last, and it was time for me to shift attention elsewhere. My several sessions here in recent time were pleasant ones. My rod of choice had been a mid-flex 8'4" three-weight. My basic strategy had been to simulate a heron's stealth, and to rap my knuckles on a log for luck.

Philosophically, my preference to stay focused on the limestone water gave sway to other dreams. Although the coming season would see me traveling southward on a few occasions, pausing for enjoyable fly-casting sessions on the famous limestone waters such as the Letort Spring Run, Big Spring Run, and Mossy Creek, I was feeling the call to visit my northern freestone waters, more than ready for a change.

Blue Ridge Buffer

1

As a new fishing season opens like the blossoming of hills and valleys close to home, I prepare for another fly-fishing visit to the Blue Ridge Mountains of Virginia and reflect on how and why I went there in the first place.

Back in the late 1970s I spent four years in northern Virginia, along the Shenandoah River at the base of the Blue Ridge Mountains. I didn't fly-fish at the time but I got to know the mountains rather intimately through my frequent visits to the nearby Appalachian Trail. I didn't have family connections in the area, but through my work at a private school I met my wife-to-be, and she had family in northern Virginia. Eventually I got a solid introduction to the northern section of the state.

Later, I moved back to upstate New York. When my son grew up and eventually migrated south to Arlington and the Washington D.C. environs, my visits to the region increased significantly. In 2012, I started to fly-fish the mountain streams of Shenandoah National Park, as well as the limestone waters of the southern district. The Blue Ridge Mountains and the trout streams of Virginia began to form a backdrop to my family and personal history.

As a northerner from upstate New York, I look back to my origin as a Blue Ridge angler and see it as one might view an autumn migration of birds. In the mind's eye, swallows migrate southward, not away from their swallow lives or as if to escape their summer homes, but toward a place their bodies know instinctively when winter grips the north country. My motive was to experience and understand a southerly home for native brook trout, and to do that in the context of enjoying an extended family life near the Blue Ridge of Virginia. I was moving from a known place to the heart of something new, at least from the angling perspective.

In my case, the Blue Ridge is a northern angler's buffer zone – a place where the old and the new blend together and interact like voices of friendly neighbors. It's a place where wilderness and civilization can exchange an understanding look at each other. I like to think that anyone can find and then appreciate a special place like this, a buffer zone of body and spirit where meaningful communication and peace are fished for and successfully landed.

2

Charlottesville, Virginia. A comfortable, November holiday. My son and I drove out from a family gathering to inspect the brook trout water in the Blue Ridge Mountains. We traveled westward from the city, passing through the lavish and rolling farm estates before stopping to park our vehicle near a reservoir just downstream of Shenandoah National Park.

I had heard from the local Orvis shop that the fishing would be only fair, if that, because of an extended drought, but all I wanted was to get out into the back country and feel the freedom of wading in classic brook trout territory. Family gatherings at holiday are incomparable, but it sure felt good to briefly shut away the rush of auto traffic, to forget the sound of television noise and the beeping nonsense of the digital realm.

I suited up for seven-foot fly rod action. My son prepared for a hike beyond a point on the trail where I would drop down to the stream. We were learning that the trail system in the Blue Ridge is extensive. Here it paralleled the native trout stream and eventually connected to the Appalachian Trail and Skyline Drive.

The stream was low but the water seemed healthier than when I saw it back in August. I pressed a strike indicator on the leader well above the bead-head nymph. The tapered leader had a 6X tippet, fine enough for this clear stream tumbling through a hollow from the ridge. I quickly got to work. It wouldn't be long before my son returned from his hike. At that point, we would head back for our rendezvous with roast turkey, vegetables, wine, and pie.

I waded upstream, careful not to spook the fish, stepping up and down the rounded boulders, thankful for the cleated bottom of my wading shoes. The farther I climbed, the better this rivertop appeared. There were shallow flats where occasionally I would spook a hefty trout, but the deep pools and riffles were a physical counterpoint for me, a balanced system that had magnets for my steely eyes.

On the following day (Black Friday), I was on the stream again, doing what came naturally. There had been no camping out at Best Buy early in the morning. There had been no rush to stampede for a hot deal on a television. I was coming back to the park where I had finished my casting one day earlier. Again, the weather was autumn perfect. Economics and political trim were far downstream.

Catching up to a pair of hikers on the trail, I joined in the viewing of a young black bear foraging on the oak-leaf carpet. Shortly after, I dropped down to the stream beyond the "second ford" and fished my way for two miles into the scenic back country.

I was thankful to have gotten an early jump on the day. Had I started any later, I may not have seen the bear nor had as much luck fishing. With an army of trail walkers in the afternoon, my hope for peace and quiet got booted like a kick to the seat of my waders. But Shenandoah is a busy national park, and you had to give these people credit. Granted, some of them probably couldn't read the regulations posted on or near the access points, and thus allowed their dogs to run unleashed through an angler's pool, but at least they weren't out shopping all day long and overstimulating the economy. And the angling pressure could have been worse. I was possibly the only person casting for wild brook trout on this Black Friday stream, although I did see a few anglers casting for stocked trout down below the reservoir.

The fishing wasn't great but it was pleasurable. The stream is slowly recuperating from a devastating "one-thousand-year flood" in June 1995 when landslides nearly decimated the native trout and other wildlife here. My appearance on the stream certainly wasn't helping the natural recovery, but to see such vast improvement from a wreckage that occurred nearly 20 years earlier gave me faith in what nature can accomplish if we allow it to heal without imposing our own self interests.

3

Driving west from Warrenton, VA into the Blue Ridge Mountains and Shenandoah National Park provided a pleasant spring reentry into the realms of hiking and brook trout fishing. My wife and daughter were good company and lent a sense of comic relief for this sunny day adventure.

On foot, we descended from Skyline Drive into the headwaters of the Rose River, a feeder stream to the Robinson that, in turn, feeds the Rapidan and, eventually, the Rappahannock and the James River system of the Chesapeake drainage. With an easy 1.3-mile drop to the Rose, I started casting for native brook trout with my conveniently designed 4-piece rod. The upper Rose was flowing clear and cold (45 degrees F., a bit chilly for dry-fly fishing but good for a bead-head nymph). Although groups of hikers and even a bait-casting fisherman were ahead of me at some of the pools, I did okay, considering I angled for only an hour or so.

The brookies were colorful and lively. My cranky legs and ankles reminded me that winter had lasted too long and that the body needed toning. The wet rocks and boulders trained me for the coming days. My wife, recovering from minor back surgery, was pleased to find that her 2.6-mile hike was covered comfortably.

On day two of this visit, I noted that March took its leave like the proverbial lamb. It was another day that I'd been waiting for all winter. The drive west from Charlottesville toward Shenandoah National Park was filled with the anticipation of high spring, of a mythic buffer zone between the Earth and Heaven.

The hiking trail along the river was starred with wildflowers, my first of the year—coltsfoot, bloodroot, hepatica, and spring beauty. Songbirds, including the Eastern phoebe and Louisiana water-thrush, rang their notes from the cliffs of this cold mountain stream.

With water temperature in the high 40s, it seemed reasonable to start casting with a nymph again. There were midges over the stream, but the stoneflies and Blue Quills had yet to make an appearance. Whereas a Hare's Ear nymph was all I really needed for the day, I was glad to mix in some dry-fly fishing after the first trout rose to the surface.

The North Fork Moormans, suffering a devastating flood, along with landslides, in 1995, seems to be making a remarkable recovery, if the size and number of its wild brook trout are any indication. Two of the trout I caught and released, fooled by an artificial nymph, seemed notable for an eastern mountain stream. The smaller specimen measured 10 inches, and the larger native was close to a foot in length.

This trout stream tumbles down the eastern flank of the mountains. There were times, well inside the park, when I wandered farther from the trail than usual. I came to places that often included a deep lovely pool, a site that offered total solitude. They were places truly problematic if I happened to break an ankle or a leg while dodging logs and slippery boulders, but I was glad for the opportunity of finding them.

On day three, April dawned cooler than the last few days of March had been, but the lower Rapidan River was alluring. I walked the river trail with my wife, daughter and brother-in-law, parting company for a while at the junction with the Staunton River. The Staunton's flow was high enough to thwart all hikers without appropriate footwear. I crossed it and proceeded up the Rapidan as residues of our larger human society began dissolving in the clear deep holes and boulder-studded pools.

With water temperatures in the high 40s again, and with bright sunshine overhead, the fishing was slower than on the Moormans, at least for a while. Drifting a bead-head nymph, I caught an occasional brook trout, but no fish would surpass the nine-inch mark today.

Day four was spent revisiting the North Fork with fair success, and day five found me once again on the Rapidan. The sky was overcast, this final day, and hung with mist and light showers. While the air temperatures climbed into the 70s, the river temp hit the lower 50s.

I fished the lower Rapidan inside the park, changing my approach from an attempt to cover new ground to slowing down and simply enjoying whatever pools and riffles were in front of me. Once more, bloodroot flowers adorned the trail edges, and the shrill piercing notes of the tail-wagging Louisiana water-thrush accompanied my efforts along the stream. I didn't see another human till the afternoon, and then only a few hikers and one other fly-fisher.

The angling was slow at first—a brookie here and there, falling to a Hare's Ear and Black Stonefly nymph and then returning (as legally required) to the water unharmed. Around noon, however, I noticed the first mayflies hatching, to be imitated by the Blue Quill and Quill Gordon dry fly patterns, and the fun began.

I wandered up the Staunton River, a Rapidan tributary, a wild and rocky stream that yielded a couple of small brook trout on an attractor pattern, but the Rapidan itself was where the catch was good. Fish rose eagerly to a Quill Gordon, size 14. My only question was, did the river hold any trout larger than, say, nine-inches long? Experimenting with various river locales, I finally answered in the affirmative.

Casting from one precarious spot above the boulders into a deep and turbulent hole, I found the trout repeatedly rising and slashing at the dry fly. It was a challenge landing them above the rocks, where I had to work them through a watery chute, but I fooled several fish as good as any from the Moormans. Bragging rights? None whatsoever. Most of the trout were fooling *me,* the angler who thought he might catch them. Obviously, the fish had other ideas.

I felt pleasantly exhausted as I hiked out of the park in the evening, ready to battle the traffic of urban Charlottesville. The following day, the sixth day of this Blue Ridge visit, wasn't likely to surpass the previous day's angling mark, so I had no problem hanging up the rod to hit the trail with friends and family. You know, going out to the breweries and wineries and barbecue joints. It's been said more than just a time or two before—this sport called fly-fishing, this passion, this way of life, means more than simply catching fish and keeping count.

Water Dog

1

We who fly-fish, hike, hunt, or otherwise make use of our natural resources, often feel grateful that we have such wonderful streams and landforms at our beck and call. Subsequently, we may hope to give a little something back to nature as a way of saying "thanks." Something almost anyone can do to help improve an ailing world is to assist the natural healing process on or near our waterways.

Whether on public or on private land, many of our nation's streams have been damaged by the push of civilization. The hand that hurt the small stream in the past can assist it in the healing process of the present. Since I'm only an amateur when it comes to stream remediation, I won't get technical here, but I'll offer a few pointers based on my experience with New York and Pennsylvania conservation groups – a small stream repair kit, if you will, a low-impact model for the soul.

Let's say you're fishing a stream in the spring or in the fall. You can clip off a few willow stalks, strip the leaves and push the stalks well into the soil or mud with a downstream slant. That is an important step that anyone can take who walks the flowing path. Another step for anyone interested is to pick up a token piece of litter each time that you visit the stream and pack it out. Start doing this regularly and you're guaranteed to get depressed as time goes on—you're keying into garbage, and you realize it's everywhere that people breathe, drink, drive, and wander mindlessly. Garbage covers the earth and even filters into wilderness regions but, as the sages have suggested, "every litter bit helps."

On a broader scale, an organization you belong to can perform a major cleanup. My chapter of Trout Unlimited has successfully sucked up several clandestine landfills that had spilled into otherwise gorgeous little brook trout streams, as well as our home river. At one location, the collected automobile tires alone weighed 2.5 tons.

To paraphrase a writer friend who also fly-fishes, I want to remember that the message of water, especially moving water, falling water, is not so much gravity as it is *renewal*.

The Upper Genesee Chapter of Trout Unlimited (TU) has been planting trees, primarily small willows but other species as well, for years. To plant trees along a stream on private property requires landowner permission, of course, but we've always found that aspect of a planting project to be relatively easy.

Willows grow quickly, hold the soil, provide some shade and add nutrients for trout and stream inhabitants. In New York, trees are available free of charge from the state Department of Environmental Conservation (DEC) for interested groups such as TU. The trees are generally available for plantings in April or May.

For larger projects such as the installment of log deflectors and mudsills on waterways that will benefit by their placement, you will need outside help, but the satisfaction gained by this labor should outweigh the hours of planning and the sweat involved. For our TU chapter's work on a headwater stream near the New York/Pennsylvania border, we got landowner permission to construct four work-sites on the stream. I requested and received assistance from a regional fisheries biologist at the DEC who helped us design the project. It takes a while to obtain the legal permits for this kind of work, but looking back on it now, I know the energy involved was worth the effort.

When you're focused on stream work your success should fly you like a wood duck over tranquil marshes. Here's a caveat, though: You'll suffer the occasional setback in remedial projects of this sort, a heartbreak that can drop you like an autumn goose on Chesapeake Bay.

Recently I drove up to our project area on the headwaters stream and was shocked to find that beavers had moved in over the winter and found a singular stand of alders, which was neatly converted into a lodge. The beavers' settlement apparently was an inspiration to construct a dam on this brook trout water. A newly formed pond had completely drowned out the hundreds of small trees that we had planted there the season before. So yes, two steps forward, one step back.

2

Early June. After weeks of rain, the sun finally dominated the sky. It was time to work on the headwater stream. My long hours of planning and preparation, leading the efforts of my TU chapter, had come to this—a Friday morning with a purpose. We were here not to further the fishing interests of anyone involved, but to assist native brook trout and other wildlife in a headwater near my home. As I found in retrospect, the project would be both challenging and spiritually rewarding.

My daughter Alyssa volunteered to document the event with a simple camera. A friend donated morning time and the use of his tractor, the only form of heavy machinery used in the project. He would chain the locust logs that were laid out in the staging area and drag them to the stream sites. Other than that, most of the work was done exclusively by hand, thus minimizing our negative impact on the trout environment.

The fisheries biologist at the New York State DEC had lots of experience with stream remediation work, and his assistance with the site designs was essential. Another dozen volunteers from our small chapter of Trout Unlimited rounded out the labor force for our work on the remote tributary, a small native trout stream flowing northward into New York from the Pennsylvania fields and forest.

When our DEC man and his assistants started preparatory work at the lowermost site, I took a smaller crew to site 4 at the upper end of our project area. There were fallen hemlocks there that needed to be sawed and dragged into place.

Mike had overseen the cutting and hauling of logs. Most of the wood employed for our work was locust, which is hard and rot-resistant. Mike had cut the locust trees on a Naples farm site about an hour away from our stream. The logs had been measured for lengths of eight, 10, and 12 feet, with an average diameter of about a foot. The logs at site 4 were exceptional, being hemlock wood that was cut on site, a preparation that saved us from otherwise hauling the heavy locusts upstream into the forest.

One big hemlock, though, needed to be dragged downstream to site 1. Mike and I prepared the 24-footer that would function as a cross-channel log embedded at an upstream angle. Its open end would connect the terminal points of two revetment logs along the eastern bank, and each log would be pinned securely with lengths of rebar.

It seemed reasonable to assume that a 24-foot hemlock trunk would be easy enough to manage for a group of six workers, including my young daughter, Alyssa. After all, we were using log-carriers as tools, and the distance was only 300 level feet, along with a few stream crossings thrown in. But five guys and one woman had their hands full and their shoulders slumped with this carry. The ground seemed to grow into our backs, and the path grew narrower with every step taken.

The long hemlock was eventually installed at its appropriate angle and with its western end embedded one-foot higher than its eastern end. Fiber mat was laid down on its upstream side. Rocks were backfilled, and stakes of live willow shrubs were planted at the log ends to encourage new growth.

The stream began to flow across the transverse log, pulling itself toward the east bank where revetment logs would be undercut, providing new shelter for native brook trout. These fish, here and elsewhere throughout their original range in eastern North America, are threatened by dangers such as global warming and habitat destruction, so our job, as I saw it, was to help them out.

The stream began its own work for the trout by scouring a deeper pool at the junction of the logs at all four work sites in our project area. The water would become more oxygenated; the silt would be pushed from the streambed, thus exposing fresh gravel for the spawning of trout here in the headwaters.

3

We labored at sites 2 and 3 all Friday afternoon. On Saturday morning, I greeted new arrivals to our staging area and proceeded to the stream. We were a small crew but I was thankful to have several Boy Scouts and their leader among us. Hopefully we'd be able to finish our job by noon.

George, a chapter member, and Joe, a retired DEC biologist, were already pounding rebar at site 3. Thinking of the motivation behind the work for this project, I presumed that it was different for everyone involved. No doubt the bottom line for each of us was the sense that we were working for native trout and their environment rather than for any self-based reason or fishing opportunity.

I doubted that anyone would ever want to fish this little stream, other than myself on an occasional basis in early spring, and then mostly on stretches farther downstream. This stretch of the water was tiny, challenging, and too far from the road for most anglers (not to mention being on posted property). From my perspective, though, all of this was part of the stream's appeal. With landowner permission, I'd been studying the stream's pools and riffles and sampling them with a fly rod for years. The fact that this brook is as remote from "civilization" in New York as any waterway outside of the Catskills or Adirondack Mountains was a major part of its appeal to me as an angler and a naturalist.

So, I checked on my own motivation for involvement here. I had been rereading a favorite American Western novel, A.B. Guthrie's *The Big Sky*, first published in 1948. Believing that the impetus for westward expansion in nineteenth-century America, as reflected in the novel, is still at work in our collective psyche, I recalled the story's main character…

Boone Caudill and friends were forging into Rocky Mountain territory in the 1830s, and they met up with Caudill's Uncle Zeb. The friends explained to Zeb that they, too, intended to be mountain men free to do as they pleased, despite their eastern upbringing. Uncle Zeb declared that they had… "better be borned ag'in." How so?

Zeb, the western mountaineer, told the young travelers they were "Ten years too late… She's gone, goddam it! Gone!" And what was gone? The country.

"The whole shitaree. Gone by God, and naught to care savin' some of us who seen 'er new."

If the beautiful land and water with its bison and beaver were already slipping away in the 1830s, Boone and friends weren't buying it. Yes, forts had already been built along the Missouri River and greenhorns were arriving quickly, slamming up against the Indians, but the friends of *The Big Sky* had a vision, like the earlier vision held by Uncle Zeb. As Zeb expressed it, "She was purty once't. Purty and new, and not a man track, savin' Injuns, on the whole scoop of her."

Boone and friends demurred, responding to Zeb by saying, "She ain't sp'iled… It depends on who's lookin'." So, the company moved westward despite the tragedy and hardship certain to follow.

Guthrie's incredible portrait of the western movement in American history had an application here at the trout stream in New York, at least in my case. I'd been monitoring the stream environment for years. I felt like a waterdog, the monitors who regularly check on regional trout streams for potential problems caused by the fracking of Marcellus Shale to unlock the gas deep inside the earth.

Waterdogs keep their eyes on the streams and rivers, ready to report a problem caused by controversial drilling methods or by other sources.

It was easy to identify, in part, with the character Boone Caudill, who had a vision of the wilderness that was. I understood, however, that what was here and now, a mere sliver of the wild, could never revert completely in our time.

The wild country had been minimized, to say the least, and yet wildness remained. You could see it there, if you stepped aside and looked. We couldn't afford to lose the little that remained.

The small-stream volunteers had taken a step aside from their usual lives to give the headwaters a helping hand. With luck, a few souls in some future generation might also step aside and see it as the water looked today.

The Cedar Run Experience

1

Since completing the fishing and hiking project that I call "The Slate Run Odyssey" about four years ago, I'd begun to consider doing a similar project with some variations on neighboring Cedar Run, a sister stream of the famous Slate. This new experiment would have its own set of challenges and, hopefully, a multitude of fine rewards, as well. Cedar Run has its source in the mountains well above the recreational hamlet of Leetonia, Pennsylvania and empties into Pine Creek that flows to the West Branch Susquehanna River nearly 12 miles later.

Again, my hope was to fly-fish the entirety of a stream in this most rural area of the state, to become more knowledgeable about a waterway that drains state forest land and offers some of the finest trout fishing in the region. I wanted to become familiar with the rugged essence of this run, to enjoy the beauty emanating from its various pools, riffles, ledges, and cliffs.

To begin with, my goal was to fly-fish the 7.2 miles of Cedar Run from its mouth upstream to Buck Run, the distance regulated as Trophy Trout fishing water. If all went well, I could then continue fishing my way upstream through the headwaters for additional mileage to a source on Cedar Mountain.

As with my initial experience on the Slate Run trek, I'd been fishing Cedar Run sporadically for 25 years, making three or four visits annually and often fishing the same familiar slots, but I didn't have a clear view of its overall character. When I recently fished the whole length of Slate Run in a one-year period, I found that my experience there had helped me better understand that beautiful stream, so I was looking for a similar education at Cedar Run, a stream roughly 10 miles north of Slate.

For this adventure, I didn't plan to push myself as hard; I could take upwards of two years to finish the climb. I'd allow myself more flexibility in the use of fly rods and equipment; I'd investigate feeder streams if I wanted to. In short, I planned to enjoy the excursion as much as possible, to take whatever time I needed, and still stay focused on my goal.

2

I began late in the afternoon of a Memorial Day weekend. I started out with a few obligatory casts on Pine where Cedar Run pours in along the western bank. Pine Creek was looking good. Kayakers were drifting by; anglers could be spotted here and there. A woman wearing a bikini shot by in her kayak 30 feet from the end of my fly line only moments after a sizeable trout spit a Green Drake dry fly from its mouth. Getting refocused, I retreated from the carnival atmosphere of Pine and stepped confidently into the cold, freestone tributary known as Cedar Run.

Singular mayflies were hatching from the run. The water temperature was a cool 53 degrees. I quickly caught a small brookie and a brown trout on a dry fly, size 16. Beyond them at the head of a pool, another trout rose to a Sulphur dun and battled with amazing energy against the rod and the prospect of the landing net. With a quick photograph, the trout was released to swim again, and the old streamwalker had begun another modest journey.

3

Five days later I returned to the run and resumed the fishing at a point where I'd left it on the weekend. There were mayfly spinners laying eggs on the surface of pools, and I braced myself for some exciting opportunities but the morning air began to heat up quickly and a change of weather was about to make itself known. The spinner fall was done in minutes and the trout activity became invisible.

Holes #1 and #2 (imaginatively named!) produced nothing for the angler despite their apple-green allure and classic stream embellishments, a natural structure reminiscent of the larger pools on Slate Run. Later in June and July, when Pine Creek begins to warm excessively, many trout seek the cool water of feeder streams like Cedar Run and find sanctuary in the depths of pools like Hole #1 and #2. They'll be difficult to catch and probably should be left alone. These are classic freestone pools with cliffs at one side and with deep riffles at their head.

After several hours of very slow fishing I retreated from the hot and humid air and walked through the woods while swatting gnats and mosquitoes. Everything had not been lost. I'd seen tiger swallowtails fluttering over the rapidly flowing stream. Louisiana water-thrushes whistled shrilly from the cliffs. I met a fly-fisherman and his young son who were also in the hot pursuit of trout. They informed me of their fishing camp near the headwaters at Leetonia and they helped me lay out a plan for my next visit to the stream. What I lacked in trout today I made up for with connections.

A mile-long gorge lay ahead of me, a difficult stretch to access because the narrow Cedar Run Road was carved from the forest well above the stream. The run put on its wilder face at this location and reminded me strongly of its neighbor, Slate Run. My small map of the stream suggested that the Blue Pool would appear about half way through the gorge; I would try to make the Blue my next destination.

4

I decided that "freedom" was my operative word while fishing Cedar Run so I allowed myself some flexibility when it came to planning all activities there. For the summer meeting of the Slate Run Sportsmen club, I presented a program based on my "Slate Run Odyssey" adventure, and afterward I learned that my friend, Dale, the vice-president for the group, had yet to fish on Cedar Run. I suggested that we look at the stream and have a go at it.

The gorge with its Blue Pool wasn't a place for an introduction when time was a factor, so I took Dale and my wife, Leighanne, upstream to the first road crossing. There, near Mine Hole Run, we fished about half a mile of stream. The rocks and cliffs that we encountered brought my fishing companion to inquire half-jokingly: "Did you bring your rattlesnake repellent?"

Although rattlesnakes are found occasionally on Slate, I had yet to hear of them being found along Cedar Run, though I admitted the possibility.

Lacking a reptilian nature, I had to ask, "What does snake repellent smell like?" Surely it wasn't like the redolence of dame's-rocket blossoms found along the stream, one of the sweetest late-spring odors imaginable. Maybe it was more like something that repelled *humanity*, I thought, something that could hold back the increasing number of recreation seekers pushing to get on these remarkable waters.

We were fishing along the run when I learned that I had left my vest pocket open and that an Orvis box filled with tiny flies was missing. This outing on Cedar was beginning to look exceptional, but not in the best of ways.

My wife had stayed back at the vehicle to catch up on crochet work. She joined us on a mission nearly impossible—retracing our earlier steps along a feeder stream where we approached a little waterfall. With eyes fixed on the ground and water searching for a foam box with flies, I tried to calculate the hours spent tying one or two hundred artificial flies in sizes down to #24, and my head just swam. But this was an adventure in exceptions, right? I found the fly box. It was camouflaged on the forest floor.

The wild browns were extremely wary in the low pools with surfaces wrinkled by conflicted currents.

The fishing was slow for early June but the sights were beautiful. We caught a few small trout near the Long Branch Pool where Sulphurs hatched sporadically, as did Grey Foxes, Slate Drakes, and several varieties of stonefly.

5

After a full day of meeting with the Slate Run Sportsmen group and doing map work for Slate, I needed to unwind, if only for an hour or so. The main difference between Cedar Run and Slate is that the former has a gravel roadway along much of its length, and thus is more accessible to an angler with limited time to spend.

I parked the car on the forested mountainside, suited up and found a short path to the run. The Tumbling Run Pool is a long, deep basin under a shelving cliff, significant even when Cedar Run is flowing low and clear. Several trout were sipping insects at the surface here, but my long casts with a 3-weight line were not producing. Only when I fished the smaller pools and riffles, above and below the big pool, did I get some action with a bead-head nymph.

I moved up to an open section lined with willow trees. Here the run was minimal, its water temperature 60 degrees Fahrenheit – not bad for mid-afternoon at the height of summer. The run was narrower than it was inside the forest, and its riffled pocket water dodging through the rocks and boulders gave an excellent opportunity to tempt wild browns with a floating Black Ant, the finest of rivertop terrestrials.

It was a good choice, and with a careful upstream stalk, I managed to deceive several nice fish including one 12-incher whose sudden appearance in the narrow stream cleansed the bloodstream of a veteran angler in dramatic fashion.

Back at the parking area, I met a couple of bamboo-wielding first-timers from Cincinnati who were friendly and inquisitive about the run. I didn't mind giving them a tip or two on where and how to find some action. Cedar Run had been generous to me, so far, and I felt sure that these anglers would treat her with respect. It seemed like a good exchange.

6

The mid-November day was unusually beautiful, sunny, warm, and still—perfect for a visit to the Blue Pool on Cedar Run. The pool I had dreamed about so early in my quest had still not been reached. I had detoured around the lower gorge in summer when I fished with Dale, and it was time to make my introduction there.

A little extra care was required. Like any wild stream, Cedar Run has its darker aspects that are generally ignored when fishing is at its best. For instance, I knew of an angler who, fishing by himself after leaving word with others about his destination, tumbled off a cliff in the lower gorge and broke his leg. He spent a cold night alone in the wilds before a search party found him later the next day. And then there was the time when I nearly lost an eye while fishing upstream near the mouth of Fahneystock Run. The darker aspects—not to be forgotten or ignored completely, if we want to continue enjoying the sublime elements of a place.

I had recently been reminded of the writer Roderick Haig-Brown, his words that, "… rivers remain places of enchantment and the fish that swim in them creatures of wonder. Some small share in this is the fisherman's real reward." What I wanted this day was something of that *reward* and not some kind of ironic pay-off. I was looking for something like an observation of a brightly colored trout, a lonely mountain view, a glance at an autumn blossom or an otter or a migratory bird. What I didn't need was the discovery of a broken-down vehicle, a shattered ankle, or some event approximating biblical proportions.

My immediate goal was to find that elusive pool suggested clearly on my small topographic map designed for fishermen. So, I descended into the gorge to a point where I had finished angling earlier in the year. I assumed that the pool was about a mile upstream in the gorge and that there was no other way to get there than to wade against the flow and to revel in the crisp, golden air.

Casting a bead-head nymph I managed to fool a couple of browns and a brook trout. I came to a flat section of woodland crowned by massive white pines. Cliffs of shale rose abruptly on the water's opposite side. It was the first in a series of three fine pools shadowed by the slopes. Small trout darted for cover in the lower pool; a pair of spawning browns (one of them perhaps 15 inches long) got spooked in the middle pool, and then at the upper end I saw the unexpected…

A huge wild brown swam slowly for the safety of ledges deep within the blue-tinged water. I stepped in slowly to the level of my knees and made a few delicate casts, knowing there was no chance of a hook-up now, but doing so in tribute to the largest trout I've ever seen in this section of the state.

I would have to schedule a return in spring, come hell or turbulent water. With the vision of a two-foot behemoth swimming around in my head, I began the long walk back to where I started from.

Later in the day, I parked along the narrow gravel course and strode into the water, ready to fish for maybe one more hour. Lifting the bamboo rod for a back-cast, I didn't know the fly was caught on a branch or a rock lying on the ground. The tip of the rod splintered and snapped in two. Talk about ironic pay-offs… I felt the stab of recognition because I'd broken rods before when tired or frustrated, but I didn't curse myself for the blunder this time, at least not as loudly as might be expected. The break would prove costly, but I was feeling too good about the day to get upset. I could work at getting a replacement tip over the winter.

For now, it was good enough to think about the real reward. The earlier day had been a pleasure. Although the culmination of events held a certain irony, I paid for it with a minimum of grief.

7

I was slow getting around to Cedar Run the following year. I didn't get there till mid-season, but when I did return, it felt great to resume my year-old quest to fish the whole length of this remarkable stream. The small bamboo rod that I'd broken in November had been repaired and I was anxious to carry on the upstream journey bit by bit.

I needed to return to the Blue Pool, but this time from the upper end so I could cover half a mile of water that I hadn't yet seen. Entering at Tumbling Run, I fished down to a pool called Little Blue. My map indicated that Little Blue was still half a mile from the larger pool, and that's as far as I got on this occasion. The weather was becoming hot and humid and the clouds looked dark and threatening. I promised myself that on the next visit I would fish the stretch between the Blues and then be ready to push toward higher ground.

The stream was in good shape for late June, with plenty of water and a temperature in the low 60s. Despite the presence of a gravel road somewhere in the woods above, I sensed a touch of wildness in the gorge. The dripping cliffs, the large white pines, the chattering of a winter wren, all of it seemed to penetrate me and provide a fix of wildness that allows me to feel more than a lame monkey or homunculus in a world of commerce.

I thought of the concept called "independence" and its connection to the imminent U.S. holiday. Being on a stream like this felt like being free, but freedom is a relative word describing our potential for making choices. I felt a love for this place where politics and patriotism did not enter, but where behavior and imagination were accounted for.

The fishing was slow, as can be expected in early summer, but I managed to catch and release five wild trout, four browns and a brook, all rather small but brightly colored. I saw a group of four mink hunting along the rocky bank beneath a cliff. The four members of the weasel family bounced among the rocks, reversing their course and then proceeding upstream once again, perhaps enjoying the day like a wayward human with a fishing rod.

A porcupine stood dining among the grasses near my feet. I moved for my camera in a vest pocket, and the porky headed for the nearest tree. I doubt that it enjoyed being interrupted at its meal. I took a couple of photos and returned to my fishing. The *quillmeister* backed down from its tree and headed for deeper woods.

Two minutes later I was in the stream, fiddling with fly and leader, when I heard some rustling at my back. Porky? Perhaps with a couple of bully friends to confront me? I turned to see a young fly-fisher looking at me with a sullen eye.

"Oh, heh!" I uttered, giving away my shock. Seeing another fisherman here was the last thing I expected. "For a second, I thought you were a porcupine. I saw one right there a few minutes back."

This guy did not appear amused. He looked like a model angler from a new Cabela's catalogue, with vest and waders just a few days old, but one who had yet to catch a fish while dressed in this attire. "Any luck?" he asked. He still wasn't smiling. I wondered where his model-angler wife and daughter were—you know, the ones who'd be beside him on the cover of the catalogue or deep within the pages where the family-oriented accessories could be found. Mister and missus and missy, the whole "fam damily" sporting the latest gear and clothing. But maybe I was being too harsh on him. Maybe he had begged for free time today and, like myself, had gone off for some needed solitude.

He told me that the trout seemed few and far between on Cedar. I politely disagreed, saying there were plenty of wild brooks and browns; it was just a slow time to be fishing. The trout were probably napping in their version of the Day Room, watching piscine television, or playing what could pass for cards. The angler didn't crack a smile at my lameness. He just said, "This is only the second time I've fished this stream. I'm heading out."

The porcupine who became an angler walked away forever. I went downstream and hooked up with a brown that nailed my Stimulator dry fly. I thought about the four minks that I had seen along the run, and wondered if, on getting back to the car, I would see four gentlemen suiting up beside their vehicle. I would look for evidence of fur and claw. I might ask them if they'd seen anything while checking out the cliffs below. I imagined them saying, out of true concern, that maybe I should just sit down and take it easy. The mountain air must be getting to me, or perhaps I hadn't caught a trout in a very long while.

8

Returning to Cedar Run one day in early July I listened to that cornerstone of jazz, "Kind of Blue" by Miles Davis. A voice from the subconscious told me that this jazz favorite would be excellent preparation for that half-mile stretch of Cedar Run between the "Blues," and so I went with it.

168

The morning sun was just beginning its entry into the glen. The sky would be cloudless, the air temperature climbing into the 80s. The stream, low and clear, had thinned considerably from its form two weeks ago. From Little Blue down to Blue I would find enchanting water, pools and riffles alternating in subtly shifting rhythms, and I made a mental note to fish this place next spring when the major hatches reoccurred.

Small trout were rising at the upper end of Blue. What were they taking? I got no response to a Blue-winged Olive or a Pheasant-tail Nymph. The water was remarkably still. I hummed along to "Freddie Freeloader" and to "So What," too, a gentle current somewhere just sliding along and gathering force, connecting a deep pool, undercut and riffle, the framework of a Pennsylvania gorge and vast deep forest overhead.

9

I had eaten a bunch of Chinese fortune cookies, looking for a bit of wisdom I could use on my next fishing jaunt. The slip of paper with six "lucky numbers" might be useful if I was a gamer who played the Lottery—but the most practical message found was one that simply stated, "Happiness is activity."

I carried the phrase, whatever it meant, to Cedar Run. The three words became my mantra whenever I questioned myself, a theme for my latest attempt to fly-fish onward toward the source. It was a beautiful Sunday morning in September and I worked a Trico spinner but the trout weren't rising. Switching to a

Prince nymph, I finally caught a small brown or two, but that was it for a while.

At first, when I saw the little waterfall above me on the cliffs, I told myself I should climb up there—the next time I come through. Then I paused on my upstream route when I heard a little voice inside me taunt with, "What do you mean, you're going to climb up there *someday*?" I heard the three words of the fortune cookie, "Happiness is activity," so I dropped my rod and reel, crossed the run, and started climbing the gulley.

I climbed over rocks and under logs, ever careful of my footing, till I reached the small cascade and waterfall—the falls that would have haunted me for months had I succumbed to "non-activity," the falls that became another pretty detail of the whole experience. It was no less a part of Cedar Run than a large, dark-colored trout that I would spook 30 minutes later in another pool down on the run. The waterfall contained the same life spirit as that 20-inch brown trout shooting out from beneath me to the safety of an underwater ledge. Discovery of one thing always leads to another and, in some small way, the details came together here and now, completely and with joy.

I waited a while before attempting to connect with the brown, then carefully stalked to a position above its ledge. I began drifting a weighted fly, a Green Weenie, through the depths beside the underwater ledge. It was a long shot for a trout that probably wouldn't move till nightfall, but I had to try it anyway, if for no other reason than… "Happiness is activity."

In one slow cast after another, I reflected on all the bad news heard throughout the media every day, on the murder, mayhem and malaise, so empty now in the depths of the brown trout's emerald pool. Well, most of what I'd been hearing seemed empty, but a couple of beauties kept their presence here, like bubbles rising to the surface…

In a new book by Steven Hawking, the author states that the Higgs boson, or "God particle," could become unstable and cause the universe, the whole freakin' breadbasket, to collapse… Whoa, I thought, if only *all* our problems could be solved so painlessly and fast!

More frightening was a new report by the National Audubon Society, based on scientific studies. The Society had conservatively estimated that some 314 species of birds, or roughly half of all the birds in North America, are headed toward extinction, quickly, thanks to man-made CO_2 production and global warming. What it means for cold water species such as trout and salmon is equally grim.

Some of the current headlines are more than just alarming. They're demonic. Like beheadings in the name of God. Are we ready to adapt to such a world, or are we too damned busy to care? That's the kind of news that keeps me casting and pushing on in places like Cedar Run, to learn more and to share what's left of beauty, however miniscule the contribution. That's what keeps me looking for that happy place where I can fish and shake off most of life's calamities, other than the willow boughs that seem to snag every third back-cast in an open area along the run.

Today that "happy place," if you will, seemed here and now. Above the ledge where the brown trout hid and, later, along a stretch of willow trees and pocket water where the caddis hatched and where a dozen brook and brown trout rose as if with an exclamation point from the best darned fortune cookie I've ever opened.

10

I chose to delay my entry into the upper gorge for a later day, perhaps in a week or so, when the autumn foliage would be sharper, redder, and with the sun spiking the wild browns into action. For now, I chose to work a stretch of water between two bridges on the stream.

My first fly of choice was a new pattern for me, a wet Grouse and Flash. It produced nothing. My second choice was an old standard, a bead-head Prince nymph, and with that I got a strong pull from deep water… The trout was on for several seconds before the tippet snapped and the fish escaped into darkness of a dreamy pool. Alright, the trout had caught me unprepared. It was, no doubt, the biggest fish I had yet to lose in Cedar Run.

Fumbling onward over the rocky and uneven bed, I found that the upstream trout would be kind to me. They rose through Red Rock Riffle and took a Black Ant as well as a Rio Grande King. I saw several brown trout 15 to 17 inches in length. Again, all of them were extremely wary in the low September flow.

When I finally got into the upper gorge, I understood that this time I had *really* gone fishing. I was casting, listening to the music of the gentle stream, to the drumming of a grouse, the squawk of a startled kingfisher. As before, the trout were abundant but extremely skittish underneath the wooded cliffs and dripping ledges. Fishing was a slow and challenging step-by-step, often where the water narrowed into a deepened riffle or a mini-pool among the multitude of rocks and boulders.

As much as I value individualism, I'm like anyone else who figures that the journey of life is, in part, the quest for beauty. I'm a die-hard Romantic but I'm not about to capitalize the word "beauty" nor am I about to quote John Keats or another poet now. I guess that if you're lucky enough to have a passion in life, you'll know what I mean. You might pursue that passion even when you know its peak is nearly unattainable.

Take wilderness, for example. *Beauty*. It's found inside these mountains, well inside the sense of "scenery" experienced from a passing car or truck. I find it, grab it, and know—it's like taking part in the creation of an art form. To find it is like letting go and getting swept up in a dream. And once inside that place, you want it to last forever.

I came close to a 20-fish day on Cedar Run, and for that I can be thankful. Rollin' and tumbling on a mountain stream was fun. May we all get the chance to roll with it someday, with wildness or with beauty, along whatever stream will carry us through.

11

The region had just experienced its first frost of the season, and the morning air, beneath an overcast sky, was decidedly brisk. Despite some recent rain activity,

Cedar Run was still low and clear and 49 degrees Fahrenheit, a tough one to be fishing now.

I approached the deep pool near Fahneystock Run and put aside my casting for a spell. For me, this outing on the stream was special. I was celebrating, in a sense, the reprint of my fly-fishing book called *River's Edge*, and here, close to the Fahneystock Pool, was the place where I almost lost an eye while fishing close to 30 years ago (God, has it truly been that long?). I wrote about that incident in the book's chapter "Fishing the Runs" and, even now, these many years later, I still shudder when thinking about my negligence and what happened because of it. But clearly, it was time to move along...

There were several deep pools with underwater ledges in this stretch of the run, and at one of them I spooked another fish that shot out from its hideaway in hot pursuit of safety. It reminded me of a small blue submarine, a behemoth nearly impossible to catch in these low water conditions. I had some luck and some disappointments here with smaller trout, and prepared myself for what lay ahead—the upper canyon and the "Meadows," and the ghost town of Leetonia, then my destination somewhere at the headwaters on Cedar Mountain.

12

I decided I could fish half the canyon on a short autumn day and then return to the car. Anything more than that might be biting off more than I could chew. I fished a small nymph, a bead-head Prince, with some success. Again the fishing was difficult because of low clear water, but several holes, or deep pools, were productive with an upstream cast.

My favorite place here was what I call the "Slanted Rock Pool." It produced a small brook trout and a couple of nice, colorful browns. The stretch didn't feel as remote or canyon-like as I expected, though a steep rocky cliff often separated me from the road above. On reaching a stand of tall red pines, I marked the place for future reference and headed back, knowing I would soon return, but with a walk downstream from the Meadows.

I drove on to higher ground and parked near a camp at the Meadows that sent enticing smells of wood smoke into the air. I found a ledge pool in the forest where I caught two more browns that measured close to 10 inches each. These small fish put up a lively struggle against my little 7-foot, 4-weight rod.

I fished upstream and fought my way through the willow trees and alders of Leetonia, and by the time I quit at the first bridge in this little settlement of recreational camps, I felt tired but happy with the trout that I had seen.

A week went by, and I returned to the former lumbering town, which was now a place of quiet camps. There I met my friend Scott, and we quickly suited up in the season's first breath of sweeping snowfall. Inspecting one of Scott's topographic maps, I gained a little certainty and assurance about where we were headed and what we planned to accomplish.

We would fish an upstream section of Cedar, above the point where Buck Run enters and forms the top boundary of Cedar's regulated Trophy Trout water.

We would fly-fish a mile of headwaters, higher up on the run than I had ever sampled before.

With short bamboo fly rods rigged with a nymph or a dry fly, we stepped into the headwaters stream that now ranged in width from a three-foot channel, relatively deep, to about a 12-foot pool that was relatively shallow. The pools and undercuts were pleasant to fish, but there was also a lot of bedrock to be found, a place with minimal opportunity for trout to feed, shelter or to spawn on.

We covered a mile of water in the vast Tioga State Forest. Each of us caught some trout, mostly small brooks and browns, but the fishing picked up just before we had to leave the stream. The midday sun had started to warm the water, and the trout were rising to my Rio Grande King and to Scott's dry Adams.

This wasn't easy fishing. The casting lanes were often tight or non-existent due to high summer grasses, alder thickets, and overhanging hemlocks, but there were also pleasant, open glades to deal with, and the autumn scenery with its colored slopes was nothing to ignore or sniff at.

Hardly anyone ever fishes here above Buck's Run where the special regulations on Cedar Run kick in. Scott and I have a theory about why. Here and elsewhere, people like to fish the special regulations water because they know that fish must live there, and that gives them a measure of assurance and hope when the times get tough, as they will, whenever wild trout are pursued in wild places.

But the solitude found on upper Cedar Run was fine with me. Streams like this are special for a fly-fisher who enjoys a lonesome hour or a day in rugged country.

13

The autumn sun was slow to arrive in the mountain valley near Leetonia. I needed to retrieve my thread of the fly-fishing walk by starting at the lower bridge near the camps and then heading up toward Buck Run.

The clear waters of the stream soon deepened into a long, quiet pool with large rocks. A group of brown trout in the depths amazed me, but none were interested in my imitations. They were educated browns, no doubt, survivors of repeated camp outings, and several of these trout looked to be 18 inches in length.

At my vehicle, I exchanged a 6-foot Fenwick glass rod for a 7-foot cane rod and proceeded upstream. I was in for a difficult stretch of tight water, alternately wide and shallow, brushy and narrow. When I finally passed a group of old hunting camps, the sun had warmed the stream a little, and the fishing improved. The run had more undercuts and pools and, best of all, the wild browns and native trout began rising to the surface for flies. Here the brooks outnumbered the browns about three to one, but both species were a pleasure, taking soft hackles and a dry Black Ant.

I forged my way to the start of the special regulations water and observed the large culvert, high and inappropriate for trout passage, pouring Buck Run into my awareness and the closure of another fishing day. I climbed out to the road, ate a sandwich and took a drink, then hiked back to the car.

Still waiting above me on the mountain were the multiple sources of this little stream. I likened those sources to the roots of a flower or a tree supplying sustenance to an entire system of life. But as my son would tell me later, those root-like sources of the stream could beckon one to follow "as high as one can climb."

14

The mid-November sun was golden, low, and mellow with the news that winter hastened its approach. If I was to walk the upper canyon comfortably this fall, if I wanted to extend the distance that I fished on the stream this year, I had to do it now.

It was Veterans Day, a time in which we duly recognize our veterans of foreign wars. It was a time to cherish our freedoms—if we understand what freedom is, or what it means.

It was a day in which I saw a lot of trucks on the road to my destination in the big state forests of northern Pennsylvania. The trucks hauled water or fracking fluids and supported the continued use of fossil fuels and the consequent breakdown of the natural world and its climate and inhabitants.

I still depended on fossil fuels, and I saw how the expression of freedom, in the larger sense, is a joke. My voice joined the chorus of rebellion against the status quo, apologizers who were saying, sure, we try to minimize our dependence, and support alternative energies. We try…

It was a 40-minute walk down to the gray birch at the evergreens, the point on the eastern bank that I had marked while fishing upstream earlier in the season. I tied on an artificial nymph and began to work the foot of the Canyon Pool. The water temperature was a chilly 41 degrees. The wild trout lying off the main current showed no interest in the offering.

In the shadows of the run below Dam Hollow I began to think that no one ever fishes here but then… What was this? A piece of leader wrapped around a high branch. A Woolly Bugger stranded over a deep hole, the barb pinched down respectably, the hook gone to rust from the passage of time.

I reached a second big pool while heading back to my starting point earlier in the day. It had a cliff with dripping water and with hemlocks that drooped their shading presence along its rocky edges. I called it the Upper Canyon Pool, and laid out my tandem flies, a dry Elk Hair Caddis with a Pheasant-tail Nymph as a dropper. It was too cold to expect good dry-fly action but the caddis served as a guide for the fisherman's eye. Several brooks and a brown trout seized the nymph and came to hand.

A pileated woodpecker chortled from the forest just beyond, and the blue sky seemed to shine as if from the patchwork of fleeting time. The great ridges and the valleys all around me were in balance with each other, a model for human aspiration, for our thoughts about freedom and energy use. Within a month or so, this wild country would be covered by winter's blanket, and the run would take its seasonal sleep. I could hope to be here in the spring for its awakening.

15

I got a break from the weather, from the frozen days and nights of late autumn for another opportunity to fish a little more of Cedar Run. I drove to the mountain and steered my way gently toward the headwaters over an icy lane of mud and gravel. Parking near Half Mile Run, I suited up and walked the road for three-tenths of a mile to the little waterfall where I had finished my upstream exploration on a previous visit.

Pennsylvania doesn't allow bear hunting on Sundays so I felt a little more at ease—not because I thought I'd be mistaken for a bruin, but because there were fewer hunters in the neighborhood and fewer gun-toting yahoos on the prowl. I sidestepped from the roadway to the stream and knew I'd better be careful with the shelf ice and the melting glaze. It was better not to break something that is better left unbroken.

If I could fish back to the car and catch a trout or two, I'd be more than happy on this dark occasion. I'd be close to my goal of fly-fishing the entire eleven-mile length of Cedar Run. I could wrap up the "Experience" for the year and fish the balance of the headwaters in spring.

Beaver dams, ice, tall grass, and low-hung branches made for challenging conditions where the run was averaging only three to six feet in width. I caught a wild brook and a brown trout, and spooked several others, including a couple of large natives. The pool at the Half Mile culvert remained under ice, despite the warming air that peaked at 41 degrees Fahrenheit.

I hauled myself out to the car and took a few obligatory casts upstream on the other side of the road, wondering what the final mile or two of fishable water would be like when springtime rolled around once more. As a pat on the back for covering a good 10 miles of Cedar over the previous months, I drove far downstream to fish a section already familiarized, a piece of water that I felt would be productive and accessible, a small gift to myself in celebration of the holidays.

16

May. I warmed up for Cedar Run by fishing several headwater streams closer to home. Near Splash Dam Hollow I stopped my vehicle to allow a hen woodcock and her short parade of chicks to safely cross. When they all reached the grasses of the roadside, the first chick hopped onto its mother's back as if to say, "I've had it mom; it's too darn hot for this!"

The day felt oppressively warm, but the birds and the trout told me that the run was calling. A rare orchard oriole and a Baltimore oriole, together on a dead tree in a marshy glade, sang the calling with their own peculiar, liquid phrases. The brook trout sang it through their lusty slashings at the dry fly—everything seemed to blend in one holy mix, a verdant sign pointing to Cedar Mountain.

The stretch between two small bridges on Cedar Run was not for the faint of heart. It's narrow and uneven, cradled by a deep ravine. The air was humid, promising rain and thunderstorms, and the vegetation looked so rugged that I couldn't imagine entering it in winter, let alone in the middle of spring.

Parts of the jaunt felt like the mixture of a suicide mission and a holiday in heaven. There were sections that I passed because they looked like gateways to the underworld, but then there were sweet little pools and cascades giving proof of their brook and brown trout populations.

Near the upper end, I found Cedar's highest major tributary, a small feeder stream that lent me a native trout, small and pretty with dark hues of the hemlock trees. And there were bugs in the air—yellow stoneflies, graceful March Browns and the Grannom caddis. The storm threat put an early end to this initial outing and, later, while inspecting the topographic maps, I realized that I could probably fish another half mile or so above the highest bridge.

17

On the day before the Summer Solstice I entered the forest where the headwaters have roots, or freshets, that spring from the ground and work in tandem with the trees to sustain a healthy ecosystem. Here my anger at the human world began to dissipate slowly. Here was a quiet realm where I could try to think rationally and be taken aside by what is beautiful. There wasn't much room here in the forest for the stuff of hatred in the world, for the tragic outbursts of American racism or the streaks of anti-intellectualism that threatened to blur our modern life. There was no place for the negatives of human nature to take root and then outgrow the good. There was no place for the lack of critical thinking in our lives, or for the fear of life's diversity.

It was time for the light of Solstice and the wonders of a white pine/hemlock forest in the Allegheny Mountains. There was room to cast here underneath the spacious boughs, room enough for a streamwalker and his memories of a fishing hike that's taken two years to complete. There was room enough for one or two human beings and the numerous small trout living in these nooks and crannies.

It was good to come here while the rains still provided a decent flow. It was good to find clear water while the streams down valley flowed high and muddy. It was good to see that freedom could be born in a simple place like this, that the hyper-patriotism of the world (where people are blind to the quality of life beyond their own political boundaries) could be viewed here for what it is.

Small brookies slammed the Stimulator dry fly and returned, a little dazed, to the riffles and log homes of their stream. The biggest fish, a nine-inch darkly colored native, spun out from a tiny plunge-pool, the highest point on 11-mile Cedar that would offer me a temporary gift.

When the faint tracks of a forest road disappeared in a jumbled glade, I knew I had arrived. There the black-and-white warblers sang their shrill, modulated notes and hunted for bugs while creeping head-long down the trunks of larger trees. There I also listened to the *veer* notes of a veery and the *teach* cry of the ovenbird, the avian music harmonizing sweetly with the song of falling water.

Even the violence that's found in nature seemed remote at this juncture in time and place. It had nothing to do with the violence in human nature that's promoted by stupidity and a lack of critical thinking. Corporate institutions may condition people into a robotic and consumeristic life-style but, again, they had nothing to do with this singular moment perched near the summit of Cedar Mountain. Here was a place where a man or a woman could sprout wings from the backside of a fishing vest.

18

A headwater region has roots. Like the crown of a tree or an unearthed flower turned upside-down, the uppermost twigs and branches of a watershed take nourishment from the atmosphere and sky.

I had fished into that crown of roots as far as I could go. The climb had reached its end; it felt like walking on air.

It was probably time to light up a celebratory Curivari, to inhale the scent of a cigar as if it was the very essence of exploration. It was probably time to break open a Southern Tier IPA and to imbibe its hoppy flavors as if from a mountain brook.

To taste and experience a wonderful mountain stream to the best of your ability, I can only recommend keeping it all in context. Cedar Run is nestled in a winding gorge without cell phone coverage or civilized conveniences. Located in some of the wildest country in the Keystone State, it's a fine place to experience the wide horizons of nature. It's a place where you can better understand your own mortality and, as such, you should walk there with care. If we protect our natural resources, our treasures like Cedar Run, if we shield them from the greed of individual men and from baser corporate interests, these wild places will remain our gateways to a universal love and freedom.

The Dream Cast (Night Flier)

1

"The sun was down. The light which illuminated the huge clock on the Court House steeple was turned on. From several directions came figures carrying fly rods, already strung up, with jiggling wet fly droppers dancing in cadence with each step. For this group the evening meal was over, any of today's worries had been carefully laid aside for tomorrow, the important business was coming up..." [from "Night Watch" by Jim Bashline, *Pennsylvania Angler*, Aug., 1967].

Two equally flowing waters join their forces at the center of Coudersport village near the headwaters of the Allegheny River and the New York-Pennsylvania border. There the Allegheny River and Mill Creek formed a pool known, since 1865, as the Goodsell Hole. Nelson Goodsell once had a planing mill at this junction pool, and there, in 1876, he caught a "speckled trout" weighing about three pounds.

In those days, prior to the introduction of European brown trout in America, the big river junction in Coudersport was filled with native trout. In a diary written by Robert H. Pinney, a well-known Coudersport angler, it was noted that, "Father used to do some night fishing for speckled trout before 1900 and he made out alright. Wasn't much point to it, though—the brook trout were so plentiful at that time a man could catch any amount of them during the day on wet flies."

After brown trout were established in northern Pennsylvania and many other regions of America in the late 1800s, the new fish became an instant hit with bait fishermen, but these larger trout also became increasingly difficult to catch, especially with flies. As the waters of the lower Allegheny, say from Roulette down to Port Allegheny, warmed each May and June, the brown trout headed upstream for the cooler waters near Coudersport.

"There were several pools on the way to Coudersport that would hold trout for a time, but the Goodsell Hole was the principle way station. The whirlpool action in the center of this junction was to the trout's liking and here the fish would pause before making another upstream dash."

The late Jim Bashline, a renowned outdoor writer and fly fisherman who grew up on the water near Coudersport, wrote the bible for a subject I was getting interested in. I read his *Night Fishing for Trout, the Final Frontier* many years ago, but it wasn't until recent days that I decided to head downstream from familiar Allegheny headwater pools and riffles to the Coudersport area where the legend and the stories of "night fishing" unfold.

I was well acquainted with the village of Coudersport. I'd been fishing upstream of the village for years, and my wife worked as a therapist and had an office in the town. I had never taken the time, however, to trace the paths of Bashline, Bob Pinney and other angling heroes to "the greatest trout-producing pool in Pennsylvania and, for that matter, maybe the entire eastern United States." Clearly it was time for me to get acquainted.

Bashline was just a kid when he hooked up with the Goodsell Hole and its dozen or so disciples. He eventually became accepted by the dedicated night anglers only by returning to its waters "night after night after night." Eventually he wrote that the most skillful of his mentors was Robert Pinney, a "continually studying post graduate himself."

Pinney was a true "trout bum" in the modern sense of the term. He never got married, stating in his diary, "Wives that get along well with fishermen are hard to find. I never took much time out to look, so I didn't find one." Pinney was a "split-purist" fly fisherman without room for distractions. A devotee of big wet flies cast after dark, he also loved the dry fly during daylight hours and is said to have been among the first to cast a dry in northern Pennsylvania. For years, he chose to be a night clerk at the Crittenden Hotel on Main Street in Coudersport, just a short walk from the Goodsell Hole.

In 1967, Jim Bashline, then the Assistant Managing Editor at *Field & Stream*, wrote that it was doubtful any man "ever knew a single piece of water as well as Pinney knew the Goodsell Hole." That statement, assuming its veracity, was enough to pique my interest and put me on the trail of Pinney's ghost.

In retrospect, I never really saw the ghost of Robert Pinney who loved the Allegheny and the Mill Creek waters prior to destruction of the Goodsell Hole in the 1950s. It was difficult to find his traces. Sure, the evening sun still reflected from the huge clock on the courthouse steeple. But the bar at Pinney's Crittenden Hotel was inexplicably closed. I settled for a lousy substitute meal at a fast-food joint. My stroll to the former shrine, the Goodsell, was predictably morose. The concrete channels of Mill Creek and the Allegheny mingled their ghosts of past and future scenes and shot me downriver for a little fishing to salvage my day. There, I tied on a variation of a George Harvey night-fly pattern and gave it drift time as the night closed in.

As Jim Bashline said, the Goodsell Hole, from the 1920s to the '50s, probably out-fished any similar piece of water in the country. Its concentration of trout, plus its dozen select night fishermen, combined for "an annual harvest of several-hundred trophy fish—fish above the twenty-inch mark!" For years, its circular shape, its incoming flows and conflicting currents, and its 12-foot average depth created a perfect setting for the relatively new pursuit of night fishing with a fly.

Downstream, at a deep hole near a covered bridge, the late-day Allegheny gave me room to wonder. Who was this man, Bob Pinney, legendary figure of the headwater nights. What agony it must have been for Bob and his cohorts to learn that Coudersport and the Army Corps of Engineers would be eliminating the Mecca of night fishing for trout on eastern waters. To be razed in the name of Progress! Wiped out so that waters could be sluiced off quickly without regard for ecological understanding or local interest.

Standing downriver of the Goodsell Hole 60 years later, all that I could see were outlines in the dark.

2

As the writer, Ted Leeson, said so eloquently in his book *The Habit of Rivers*, the triple crafts of angling, writing and living sometimes merge as one sweet occupation. The elements merge to form a small completeness that may be only local and temporary in nature, but one whose components are equal in every way. As a writer myself, who fishes and tries to be receptive to all of angling's connections to this life, I can only nod my head agreeably. In other words, there's more to this love of the angling life than fish alone.

On the opening day of northern Pennsylvania' s trout season I resort to my personal tradition of fishing all three branches of the upper Genesee River. In a moment of poetic inspiration, I might equate the three branches to those occupations of fishing/writing/living but, more significantly, I just want to get reacquainted with these home waters after a long cold season of rest.

This year on the opener, the morning weather was already beautiful as I drove past fishermen knotted together near the bridges and stocking points. For most of my efforts this day, I was headed to higher ground, to the smaller, colder waters where, with luck, the wild fish would be thriving.

Typically, I don't catch many trout on the East Branch (aka the main stem of the Genesee), and I didn't catch one there on this occasion, but I found the visit interesting nonetheless. I like the feel of the river's farmland, now retired and reverting into forest. And I was pleased to get an electrifying jolt there from a trout living underneath a logjam.

I had worked an old streamer (a gift from a tree along upper Cedar Run) into the logjam after deciding to use it even though its hook was dull and rusted. The trout, a large wild fish or possibly a holdover that had traveled upstream from the stocking holes, struck the weighted fly and held on long enough to allow me a glimpse of its broad and colorful side…

The natural world is full of mystery and surprises. If we're caught sleeping or are simply unprepared, we'll miss out on some of that. If our senses are dulled like my streamer's hook, we'll probably lose that big fish, and there'll be no one to blame but ourselves.

I usually do my best Genesee River fishing on the West Branch. I covered several sections of it on opening day, but it was slow. I managed to bring in and release one good brown trout, but only after a deliberate change of strategy. Casting a Woolly Bugger across the water and allowing it to drift downstream, I was getting chases from trout that never connected. I tried different ways of streamer casting but nothing worked until I changed my course. As soon as I shifted from a downstream walk to an *upstream* wade and redirected my casting toward the head of pools, I started to see the light.

And that's the fun of it, of course. Just when you think you've got a handle on one aspect of the fishing game, the picture changes and you've got a new puzzle to unscramble.

At the start of the year I set up a short list of angling challenges to consider for the months to follow, and on opening day I got around to meeting one of those personal challenges when I visited the headwaters of the Middle Branch Genesee.

I'd always wanted to fly-fish on the Triple Divide itself, on the summit of the only triple watershed divide east of the Rocky Mountains. Three great river systems share a singular point of origin on this hill near Gold, Pennsylvania. I was familiar with fishing the divide just downstream on all three rivers—the Genesee, the Allegheny, and the Pine—but I'd never wet a line on the private properties at the actual summit where the flows begin.

I had wanted to fish the big divide for its native brook trout but the land is posted and I didn't see much likelihood in accomplishing this goal. Furthermore, the Middle Branch of the Genesee is tiny at its headwaters, by which I mean it's only three to four feet wide in early spring and, in places, is impounded by beaver dams and crazy avenues of alder growth.

But I got lucky. I received an invitation to fish on private property and found myself casting there on opening day.

The fishing on the Middle Branch was tough. I had to stalk on my knees and utilize a bow-and-arrow cast, along with dapping and underhand swings of the fly. And yet, the challenge had an aspect of sublimity, as well. The owners had provided a park-like character to a section of their stream, with a mowed path and log bridges for convenient crossings. I could see one birthplace of the river just upstream on a wooded slope, and I felt quite fortunate and thankful to be catching small brook trout in this location.

"Geez," remarked another angler later in the day when I told him about the place where I recently wet a line. "That's a whole 'nother world in there, and no way in hell would I want to do it."

I understood the sentiment. It's all about our attitudes and relationship with nature, how we see ourselves in the world. I enjoy not fitting in well with the norms, but I like the sense of natural community that's offered by this life, the place where human beings, bird and tree, and trout and stream all blend together in a lively configuration.

3

George Harvey, Bob Pinney, Gene Utrecht, and Jim Bashline were among the group that spurred the night-fishing game for massive trout on the upper Allegheny when the Goodsell Hole was reputed to be among the most amazing places anywhere for catching browns on moonless nights. The Hole was the place to fish for big trout when they lost their inhibitions and went prowling.

Bashline died in 1995, and Tom Dewey, an angling friend and neighbor of Jim's in Coudersport, spoke at Bashline's memorial service by the former Goodsell Hole. Dewey spoke about the days fishing here with Jim and many of his cohorts, and he spoke about the time when he was just a youngster, meeting with Jim initially and learning how to night-fish with the masters.

I once had the privilege of fishing the nearby Oswayo Creek with Tom Dewey. We didn't night-fish but I learned a thing or two from this friendly elder. Tom had once wrestled a 30-inch brown trout in a woodsy isolated pool of the Oswayo—at night, when you couldn't see the hand in front of your face. And as we fished near that same pool again, we were struck by one of the fiercest thunderstorms I've ever encountered while far from a house or a vehicle. Thinking of it now, my head reels like a test pattern on a TV screen in days of old.

More recently, I was thinking not of test patterns but of fly patterns once used on the darkened waters near Coudersport. Jim Bashline spoke about a Yellow Dun wet fly with a #8 hook, a locally famous tie that's almost entirely lost now in a proverbial thousand-page history book of trout fly patterns. Bashline had provided a skeletal recipe for the Yellow Dun in his night-fishing book, and I had tried to tie this local favorite, but my variants were unsuccessful. These flies, however, did share one thing with all the other Yellow Dun variants tied by night-fishing students— there was no obvious yellow, or dun-colored material, anywhere on the fly.

This wet fly pattern, once proclaimed by anglers to be unparalleled for meaty browns, was first tied by Caroline Phillips of Coudersport who, along with her fly-fishing husband, moved to California in 1920 and eventually sank the secret for the Yellow Dun's concoction when she passed away. Imitations abounded in Phillips' wake but nothing could really reproduce the wet fly's body of rosy mohair. The original body, when in water, is said to have appeared like "a glob of bloody flesh."

Nothing could really reproduce that natural texture—until recently.

I was contacted by James Cecelia, a self-proclaimed "wet-fly-only angler," who lives in upstate

New York. Cecelia spoke about our mutual interest in the writings of Jim Bashline and the tying of the Yellow Dun, admittedly a fly pattern that contributed to a rising fascination with the quest for big trout active in the dark.

We acknowledged that little has been written and recorded about the fly involved with the capture of huge trout in and near the village of Coudersport. All that anyone really had to build on were the following words about the local favorite in Bashline's book: The body was constructed with "…pinkish red mohair, with traces of red and yellow. When wet, it looks like raw beef, but still retains some yellowish tones."

James Cecelia had tied some exquisite-looking Yellow Dun wets and sent me a handful of the flies to test in my rivertop country after dark, and I was honored by the opportunity.

I waited for the best time to cast these wet flies in a giant Allegheny River pool below the village of Coudersport. The place was nothing much like the famous Goodsell Hole but it would have to suffice. The pool was roughly 200 feet long and was deep enough for swimmers to leap from a rope tied high above an old abutment.

Before darkness fell, the water was a fair 66 degrees, and I quickly caught a nice brown trout on the surface with an Ant. As the dusk began to deepen, I made some changes. I went to my alternative rig, switching from a delicate rod and line to a heavier outfit equipped with a brace of big wet flies—the Yellow Dun and a Governor.

There would be no moon tonight. I saw that several large fish were feeding underneath the surface and displacing water well beyond my casting range. The pool was deep, contained by steep banks dense with vegetation. My maneuverability was limited and, as night descended, I could hear occasional splash or burbling sounds that raised the hairs along my neck. It was time to make a dream cast. It was time to face what Jim Bashline called "the final frontier."

About the Author

Walt Franklin is a writer, educator and naturalist who ventures outdoors as much as he can. He is an active member of the Slate Run Sportsmen in Pennsylvania and Trout Unlimited in New York. His collection of fly-fishing essays, *River's Edge*, is in print along with three other collections, *Beautiful Like a Mayfly*, *A Rivertop Journal* and *Sand & Sage.* He has also written and published *Earthstars, Chanterelles, Destroying Angels* and several other slender volumes of poetry. He lives in an old farmhouse near Greenwood, New York with his wife, Leighanne.

Check out his regularly posted fly-fishing blog at **www.rivertoprambles.wordpress.com**

For more information about Walt's work and similar writings, visit the Wood Thrush Books website at **www.woodthrushbooks.com**